Table of Contents

Book Introduction: 6

Chapter 1: Introduction To Stress And Anxiety 7

   Stressful situation + human perception = stress response: ... 9
      Stressors: 9

   What Causes Stress in young people? 9
      School: 9
      Academic expectations: 10
      Bullying: 10
      Sex and sexuality: 12

   Main Causes Of Stress in Adults: 14
      Family conflict: 14
      Financial Difficulties: 15
      Relationships: 15
      Work : 16

   Anxiety: 16
      Types of anxiety: 17
      What you can do: 19

Chapter 2 - The link between anxiety, stress and depression: 21

   Symptoms of anxiety disorder in children might include: ... 21

   How to help yourself with your anxiety? 22
      Anxiety and Stress: 23
      Anxiety and Alcohol: 24
      Can foods treat anxiety? 25

Chapter 3 -Low self-esteem, Stress, Depression and Suicidal feelings: 26

A lifelong process: 26

Effects of low self-esteem: 27

Depression and Suicidal feelings: 28

Major Depression: 30

Persistent Depressive Disorder (Dysthymia): 31

How common is depression? 31

Symptoms of all types of depression: 32

Major Depressive Disorder (Major Depression): 32
    Symptoms of this depressive state are: 32
    Dysthymia: 33
    Psychotic Depression: 34
    Postnatal depression: 35
    Seasonal Affective Disorder (SAD): 36
    Bipolar disorder or manic-depressive disorder: 37
    Childhood Depression: 38
    Teen Depression: 38
    Double Depression: 38
    Secondary Depression: 39
    Treatment-resistant Depression: 39
    Masked Depression: 39

Causes of Depression: 40

Treating Depression: 43

Drugs vs Natural Relief: 46
    Drugs as a way of treating depression: 46
    Natural ways of coping with depression and anxiety 47

Chapter 4 - Stop and Think! Why are you sad? 50

What is bothering you? 50

Using conversation as a cure: 51

Therapy or Counselling: 52

Chapter 5 - Effects of Depression *56*

Physical: 56

Physical illness and depression: 57

Medical Illness and Depression: 57

Ways to Beat Anxiety: 58

A mindset to beat depression! 61

Chapter 6 - Setbacks, suicide and how to get help! *63*

Coping with suicidal thoughts: 65

Supporting friends and family with depression and anxiety: 67

What you should do: 67

What you should not do: 68

Signs of possible feelings of suicide: 69

What happens if they do not want help? 70

Chapter 7 - 28 Lifestyle changes to combat depression and anxiety! *71*

How to politely deal with negative people: 83

How to improve well being: 90

Chapter 8 - Self-Healing *92*

The different meanings of self-healing: 92

What is the Self-Healing Process? 96

Chapter 9 - Boost your self-esteem and create better habits *100*

Chapter 10 - Turn Negative Thoughts into Positive Ones 107

Practical Steps to counter negative thoughts: 108
Summary of practical tips to help you stay positive: 110

Chapter 11 - Feel Good activities 111

Chapter 12 - Break the chain with mindfulness meditation 117

Worry and Pre-Worrying: 117
What Is Mindfulness Meditation? 118
Getting Started: 118
Mindfulness Tricks to Reduce Anxiety: 128

Chapter 13 - Self-Confidence and Self-Belief 134

The psychology of Self-Belief and Self-Confidence: 134
The Importance of believing in yourself: 137
The Role of Self-Confidence in Relationships: 139
Road map for building self-confidence skills: 142
Steps for Boosting your self-confidence: 144
How do you stop a panic attack? 151
Understand and learn your triggers: 157
Caffeine: 158
Hunger (Skipping Meals): 158
Negative Thoughts and Over-Thinking: 158
Social events and going out in public: 159
Conflict: 160

Make a Journal: 160

Effective strategies for reducing anxiety: 161

Helping someone during a panic attack: 163

Conclusion *165*

About Me (The Author) *167*

Book Introduction:

We all go through varying amounts of stress and anxiety at every stage of our lives, our teen days, even at school, and throughout adulthood, that's why this book is perfect for whichever stage you are at in your life.

You experience new and different things, which can be both good and bad. You feel things more intensely than ever before. You are discovering who you are and what you want in life, and you are trying to figure out how you fit into the world around you. It's no wonder that many people feel stressed and anxious at times.

People nowadays have to face enormous pressure and anxiety every day. The reasons can be anything from academic achievements, plans, family expectations, social life, and many more. It has been proven by research that these pressures if not managed or coped with properly can lead to some serious psychological problems like depression and anxiety disorders.

So people need to learn some effective stress management skills to deal with their everyday anxieties. This book is written with the needs of everyone in mind. It contains useful tips and advice on how to manage stress and anxiety positively.

This book will hopefully be beneficial for all the people who are struggling with stress and anxiety in their daily lives.

Chapter 1: Introduction To Stress And Anxiety

Welcome to this introductory chapter on stress and anxiety. I'm thrilled for you that you have picked up this book as it means that you are interested in learning more about managing stress and anxiety in your life.

First, let's explore what we mean by 'stress' and 'anxiety'. Stress is our body's way of responding to any kind of demand or threat. When we sense danger—whether it's real or imagined—the body's defences automatically go into high gear in a process known as the "fight-or-flight" response or the "acute stress response".

The fight-or-flight response is a natural reaction that has evolved over millions of years as a way of protecting us from harm. It is characterized by a series of physiological changes that prepare our bodies to either stay and confront the threat or to run away from it.

The changes that occur during the fight-or-flight response include:

• An increase in heart rate and blood pressure

• An increase in respiration

• An increase in blood flow to the muscles

- A release of sugar and fats into the bloodstream for extra energy

- A suppression of non-essential body functions, such as digestion and reproduction

All of these changes are triggered by hormones, including adrenaline and cortisol, that are released by the adrenal glands.

While the fight-or-flight response is a normal and necessary survival mechanism, it can become problematic when it is constantly activated by perceived threats that are not life-threatening. For example, if we are constantly worried about an upcoming test or presentation at work, our bodies will remain in a state of high alert, which can lead to fatigue, irritability, muscle tension, and difficulty sleeping.

Anxiety is a normal stress reaction. It is characterized by feelings of tension, worry, and nervousness. Anxiety can be helpful in some situations—for example, it can motivate us to face a fear or take steps to avoid a dangerous situation. However, when anxiety is constant or excessive, it can become disabling.

When people think of stress, they often associate it with negative situations such as job loss, financial problems, or family issues. However, stress can also be caused by positive experiences such as getting married, buying a house, or having a baby.

Stressful situation + human perception = stress response:

The stress response is the body's way of protecting us. When we perceive that we are under threat, our bodies react by releasing a burst of hormones that increase our heart rate and raise our blood pressure. This "fight-or-flight" response gives us the energy and strength we need to deal with the situation.

Stressors:

Anything that causes stress is called a stressor. Stressors can be physical (e.g., noise, crowding), psychological (e.g., worries, fears), or social (e.g., relationships). They can also be external (e.g., job, school) or internal (e.g., thoughts, emotions).

What Causes Stress in young people?

School:

Chances are, the older you become, the more you will worry about school and a career. There is pressure to do well in school. Then there's the pressure associated with going to college. What schools to apply to? How to pay for school? Is it worth going to college or is it better to go right out into the job force? These are not easy questions to answer, especially for adolescents. The biological changes and other stressors can make it difficult to concentrate, yet when it comes to education and career, concentration is needed to make the right decisions.

Academic expectations:

School is considered one of the most significant stressors for students, partly due to factors discussed in the book and also because of pressure to do well in school.

What kind of expectations do you have about school?

What are your expectations?

It's bad enough for you to disappoint yourself by not doing well. It can be even worse to disappoint your parents. If too much pressure exists to do well, then there's an increased risk that you won't do as well as you're supposed to do.

The authors of one study looked at stress in both high-achieving students and those in a general education program. Not surprisingly, the authors found that students in the high-achievement group experienced more stress than those in the general education group. However, the higher level of stress did not hurt their academic achievements. This is the opposite of what other studies have shown—that more stress hurts grades.

Bullying:

No one likes a bully, especially people who are the targets. And it seems that more and more news stories focus on school bullies. Just how big of a problem is bullying? Well, depending on the information you look at, it can be a small or large problem. For example, some research by the government indicates that approximately one-third of students between the ages of twelve and eighteen are bullied. The National Youth Violent Prevention Resource Center cites that 11 per cent of students in grades six through ten are victims of bullies. Another 13 per cent are bullies, and 6 per cent are both bullies and victims.

Even worse is that bullying now happens over the Internet by sending harassing e-mails or instant messages. Creating demeaning or embarrassing Web sites about a person is another form of cyber-bullying. Online social isolation is another approach that happens when peers purposely ignore another's online presence.

Most people do not tell that they are being bullied. Research shows that people are often embarrassed about being bullied and keep the problem to themselves. Others fear they will get in trouble because of their involvement. For example, someone who bullies and is a victim of bullying will not be likely to share his problems out of fear that he'll be punished for his actions. Whatever the reason for not telling you, the result is the same: you're left in the dark.

Generally speaking, there are two types of bullying: physical and nonphysical. Physical bullying is self-explanatory—it's when the victim is hit, kicked, punched, spit on, and so on. Nonphysical involves name-calling, threats, spreading rumours, social isolation—the list goes on and on. Nonphysical bullying is more common than physical bullying, and it can leave permanent marks on your teenager.

Bullying can have serious consequences. It can cause depression and anxiety disorders to develop and can even lead some to attempt or commit suicide. In March 2010, nine people were arrested for their alleged role in driving a girl to commit suicide. They were accused of bullying the girl to the point that she took her own life. This may be an extreme example of the consequences of bullying, but it underscores the type of pressure people can feel because of it. Unfortunately, if you do an Internet search you will find plenty of instances in which victims of bullying attempted or successfully committed suicide. Almost all kids get teased or picked on at some point. You can say that's a normal part of growing up. However, there is a difference between being occasionally picked on and being bullied. Ideally, neither should happen.

Sex and sexuality:

Another source of stress for people is sex and their sexuality. As you know, puberty creates plenty of changes in the body. This includes developing sexual urges and exploring sexuality. It's not uncommon for people to initially feel uncomfortable with the changes they are experiencing.

Many teens become sexually active, despite hopes from parents to hold off. Worse, many parents are under the impression that their own kids are refraining from such behaviours while other teens are "irresponsible." However, the Centers for Disease Control and Prevention (CDC) found in 2007 that 48 per cent of high school students had already had sex, with 35 per cent currently active. You may find it even more surprising that 15 per cent had already been with at least four different partners. Unfortunately, 39 per cent of high school students do not use a condom during sex. If they develop a sexually transmitted disease or get pregnant, their stress levels will increase exponentially.

At this point, some students will also question their sexuality. Are they straight? Gay? Indifferent? Even more stressful is how their friends and family might react if they aren't straight. People who are gay, lesbian, bisexual, or transgendered (LGBT) experience more stress and are at an increased risk for self-harm and suicide. They are also more likely to be bullied and discriminated against, as the authors of one study found. Their research results showed that teenage males in the LGBT category experienced more discrimination than LGBT girls. Both LGBT males and females were more likely to experience depression, suicidal thoughts, and engage in self-harm. A 2010 study found similar results.

Compared to straight people, those who were gay, lesbian, bisexual, or unsure of their sexual orientation were more than twice as likely to feel sad or hopeless. They were almost three times more likely to consider suicide and 3.5 times more likely to attempt suicide.

Sexuality is a significant stressor for people. Think about your own experiences when you were a teenager. Were you unsure of your sexuality? Did you discover that you were gay or lesbian and didn't feel safe sharing this with your friends and family? Did others accuse you of being gay or lesbian? Maybe you knew someone who was the target of such gossip. What kind of impact did that sort of gossip and bullying have?

Main Causes Of Stress in Adults:

Family conflict:

You can pick your friends but not your family. So the saying goes when people complain about their families. I'm willing to bet that your family has conflict in it. Maybe it's not too bad or unusual. You may have regular disagreements with your teens as they try to become more independent. Maybe there are issues with your spouse, creating temporary tension and arguments—you know, the daily hassles of life. Hopefully, your house isn't characterised by perpetual arguments or violence. If that's the case, then you are under a great deal of stress, whether you realize it or not.

Conflict at home can be difficult. Home is supposed to be a safe place to go. However, when there is constant arguing or if the threat of violence exists, home can be more stressful than dealing with others at school.

It's pretty stressful for a student to have to deal with this. And this stress impacts other areas of your life. It's been shown that a stressful home environment hurts a teenager's grades, ability to concentrate, self-esteem, ability to cope in a healthy manner, relationships with other people—and the list goes on. The more severe the domestic conflict, the more problems you will likely experience in other areas of your life. And that can cause more arguments between you and your family, which adds to stress at home, which causes more problems...

Financial Difficulties:

Money worries are one of the main causes of stress in adults. Either a change in our income or a new or unexpected expense. Often financial stress is caused by even the possibility of change, the expectation that something MIGHT happen.

Often the suggestion of a "change" at work, can put fear into us. "Am I in trouble", "Could I lose my job", and often, none of these things happen, but the mere thought of them can raise our stress levels, often for weeks at a time, worrying about a potential change.

Relationships:

Relationships can be responsible for untold happiness, and also huge amounts of stress. We are not going to be suggesting what you should or shouldn't do in your relationship, (that's for a whole other book altogether!) however if you are feeling stressed in your relationship, you should communicate with your partner, explain to them how you are feeling and what is making you feel stressed and/or upset, and without a doubt, if they care about you and your state of mind, they will be supportive and happy to help you work through your feelings and barriers.

Work :

One of the most common causes of stress in adults is work-related stress. This can be either from the pressures of the job or from problems with working relationships with your colleagues. Often people that mostly work alone, can feel stressed because of all the responsibility of doing everything themselves. Repeatedly entering your body's "Fight or Flight" mode will over time cause major stress.

You can try to control some of the stresses at work by doing one or all of the following:

- Schedule regular breaks
- Pause, and take a few deep breaths
- If you can, get out and do some light exercise during your break
- Eliminate any distractions that you have control over
- If necessary, ask a friendly co-worker for some help or to take some of the workloads off you.

On top of these, make sure that you drink plenty of water and keep yourself fed during the day.

Anxiety:

Anxiety is a normal emotion that we all feel from time to time. It is the body's way of preparing us to deal with danger or threat. For example, if you are about to take a test, you may feel anxious. This is because your body is getting ready for the challenge.

One of the most common reactions to stress is anxiety. Stress can cause you to become worried, fearful, agitated, or uneasy. Physical reactions to anxiety include bodily tension, fatigue, headaches, nausea, chest pain, difficulty breathing, shortness of breath, twitching, insomnia, and more.

Anxiety can be a temporary or chronic state. Temporary anxiety is an understandable response to stressful events. Chronic anxiety is a serious problem and even takes a significant toll on the body, in which it is not working in a normal fashion. The continuing anxiety may be triggered by chronic stress, or an anxiety disorder may have developed which keeps the body in an anxious state even when no stressors are present.

Types of anxiety:

There are several types of anxiety disorders. Generalised anxiety disorder (GAD) is a common one that people can suffer from. Individuals with this disorder are chronically anxious. According to the National Institute of Mental Health Web site, generalised anxiety disorder "is an anxiety disorder characterised by chronic anxiety, exaggerated worry, and tension, even when there is little or nothing to provoke it." A diagnosis of GAD is given when a person worries excessively about everyday problems for at least six months.

Another type of anxiety disorder is obsessive-compulsive disorder (OCD). The National Institute of Mental Health says that OCD "is characterised by recurrent, unwanted thoughts (obsessions) and/or repetitive behaviours (compulsions)." Examples of OCD include repetitive hand washing, counting, checking, and constantly cleaning. Obsessive thoughts can focus on almost anything, such as being worried about coming into contact with germs, being afraid of social embarrassment, being afraid of hurting someone, and so on.

These obsessions cause people with OCD to engage in compulsive behaviours. Washing one's hands until they are raw is an example. Repeatedly checking to make sure a door is locked before leaving is another. It's common for people to make sure their door is locked when leaving; however, those with OCD will repeatedly check the door in a very short period.

Another anxiety disorder is panic disorder. This occurs when someone has unpredictable panic attacks. Nothing in the immediate area acts as a trigger for the panic. Think of it as a faulty "panic" switch that is randomly turned on. When it comes on, a person can suddenly have difficulty breathing, become dizzy, have a tight chest, break out into a sweat, faint, and so on.

Social phobia, or social anxiety disorder, is another type of anxiety disorder. The National Institute of Mental Health says that social phobia is characterised by "overwhelming anxiety and excessive self-consciousness in everyday social situations." Those with a social phobia are extremely worried that others are watching and judging them. They worry about doing anything that may be seen as embarrassing.

They scrutinise everything they wear, say, or do to avoid humiliating themselves. Social phobia should not be confused with having a specific phobia, such as a fear of flying or spiders. Both are anxiety disorders; however, social phobia causes more anxiety for a sufferer.

Post-traumatic stress disorder can occur after experiencing a traumatic event. This could be a car accident, a natural disaster, a violent encounter, and so forth. The National Institute of Mental Health says that PTSD can occur "after exposure to a terrifying event or ordeal in which grave physical harm occurred or was threatened." Symptoms involve having flashbacks of the event while awake or dreaming. Those suffering from PTSD may avoid people, places, or situations that remind them of the event. Another symptom is hyper-arousal, which refers to being easily startled or always "on alert."

What you can do:

Experiencing anxiety or suffering from an anxiety disorder can cause a lot of problems for you.

Because of all the psychological, social, and physical changes you may experience, it is easy to understand why many develop an anxiety disorder.

If you suffer from anxiety, It's important for your friends or family to keep an eye on your well-being. If you're constantly acting fearful or "edgy", then try to find out what is going on. If the appearance of anxiety or fear is chronic, you should talk with both a counsellor and a doctor. The sooner you can diffuse the problem, the better it will be for you.

Chapter 2 - The link between anxiety, stress and depression:

It is possible that if you have an anxiety disorder, you may also be stressed and depressed. While stress, anxiety and depression may occur separately, it is not uncommon for these mental disorders to manifest themselves at the same time. Clinical or major depression can manifest itself in the form of anxiety. Likewise, hitting symptoms of depression can be triggered by an anxiety disorder. However, the symptoms of both conditions can be managed with many of the same treatments. That is medication, psychotherapy or counselling and lifestyle changes.

It is natural and common for you to have anxieties. People may experience anxiety as they grow up. However, they tend to develop and learn from their parents, guardians and friends skills, to calm themselves and cope with these feelings of anxiety. It is, however, important to stress that anxiety in children could become chronic and persistent and later develop into an anxiety disorder. If left uncontrolled, anxiety may begin to interfere with the daily activities, leading to children avoiding interaction with their peers and family members.

Symptoms of anxiety disorder in children might include:

- Irritability

- Sleeplessness

- Agitation

- Feeling of isolation

- Shame

Anxiety treatments for children include cognitive behaviour therapy and medications, as well as using calming techniques to adjust their focus.

How to help yourself with your anxiety?

There are many reasons why you may be anxious, but people who feel anxious or experience symptoms of anxiety frequently may have an anxiety disorder.

Symptoms of anxiety in adults may include nervousness, shyness, isolationist behaviours and avoidance. Likewise, they may act out, perform poorly at work, and skip social events; they may also engage in substance or alcohol abuse. For some people, depression may be followed by anxiety. It is essential to diagnose both conditions so that treatment can address any underlying issues and help relieve the symptoms. The most common treatments for anxiety in people are "talk therapy", and in some longer-term more severe cases, the use of medication may help. These treatments help to address depression symptoms too.

Anxiety and Stress:

It is true to say that stress and anxiety are two sides of the same coin. Stress results from demands on your brain or body. Events and activities which you engage in could contribute to your worry, fear or unease. On the other hand, anxiety can be a reaction to your stress, and it may also occur in people who have no obvious stressful situations.

Both stress and anxiety may have mental and physical symptoms, such as:

- Stomach aches

- Headaches

- Sweating

- Dizziness

- Fast heart rate

- Agitation or nervousness

- Muscle tension

- Panic

- Rapid breathing

- Irrational anger or irritability

- Difficulty concentrating

- Restlessness

- Sleeplessness

Small levels of anxiety and stress are right for you. Both can provide you with a bit of a boost or an incentive to accomplish the tasks or challenges you face. However, if they become persistent, they can begin to interfere with your daily life. In that case, it is essential to seek help or treatment. The long-term outlook for untreated depression and anxiety includes chronic health issues such as heart disease, digestive problems, concentration, and memory impairment, to mention but a few, but these can be reduced or avoided with help and the right support.

Anxiety and Alcohol:

If you are anxious frequently, you may decide that you would like to have a drink to calm your nerves. After all, alcohol is a sedative that can depress your nervous system's activity, leading to a feeling of relaxation. In social settings, you may feel as if that is the right answer you need, to let your guard down. However, ultimately this, in most cases, is a detrimental solution. Quite often, some people with anxiety disorders end up abusing alcohol or drugs regularly to feel better. This dangerous approach can lead to dependency and addiction. It may be necessary to treat an alcohol or drug problem before addressing the anxiety. Chronic or long-term use can ultimately make the condition worse too, with extra anxiety about what happened while you were under the influence.

Can foods treat anxiety?

The most common treatments for anxiety include the use of talk therapy and medication. Lifestyle changes, such as getting sufficient sleep and regular exercise, can help massively too. Some research suggests that foods you eat may also have a beneficial impact on your brain if you frequently experience anxiety. These foods include:

- Chamomile, Salmon, Turmeric
- Yoghurt, Green tea

In cases where there is a mild anxiety disorder or a fear of something, it's often possible to easily avoid or decide to live with the condition and not seek treatment.

Chapter 3 -Low self-esteem, Stress, Depression and Suicidal feelings:

Self-esteem is one of the most important factors in dealing with stress. It can be either a source of stress (low self-esteem) or protection against stress when it arises (high self-esteem). Self-esteem can be defined as "a combination of feeling loved and capable." Others indicate that self-esteem refers to how a person thinks about themselves. The National Association for Self-Esteem says it is "the experience of being capable of meeting life's challenges and being worthy of happiness." I look at it this way: it is how you feel about yourself based on your life experiences.

A lifelong process:

Self-esteem is developed over time, from childhood all the way through adulthood. A person's self-esteem will fluctuate in response to life circumstances. For example, if you fail an exam, get dumped by a girlfriend or boyfriend, or do poorly in a sporting event, your self-esteem is going to take a temporary hit. On the flip side, if all those events have a positive outcome, the level of self-esteem will temporarily rise.

Research shows that self-esteem is generally the lowest during adolescence. This isn't surprising. With everything that is happening during this transitional period, it is easy for people to doubt themselves, at least temporarily. Other major sources of stress also play a role here: peer pressure, concerns about school and a career, bullying, sexuality, conflicts among friends and family, and going through the wonderful experience of puberty.

As we go through life, although we are still affected by these events, we tend to be able to cope with them better, as we have been there before usually, but when these events still affect us deeply, that is when we need to take action and help ourselves to discover a way to navigate through without hitting a wall.

Effects of low self-esteem:

The impact self-esteem has on you simply cannot be overstated. It influences everything—from developing and maintaining friendships to doing well in our daily lives, to medical and emotional disorders.

Low self-esteem not only influences stress—it can be affected by stress as well. Stress has a stronger influence on people with low self-esteem, and because self-esteem influences the ability to solve problems, those with low self-esteem will have more difficulty finding healthy solutions to their problems. Unfortunately, this leads to more stress, which further lowers self-esteem.

Research has shown that self-esteem influences positive and negative behaviours. The authors of one study found that low self-esteem, along with stress and poor coping skills, influences eating attitudes that can result in eating disorders. Another result of low self-esteem is depression. Further, low self-esteem affects poor coping strategies.

There is concern that self-esteem during adolescence can have long-term effects. In other words, low self-esteem during the teenage years may translate into more problems during adulthood. However, the authors of another study looked at this question of whether teen self-esteem influences adulthood and found some encouraging results.

These findings indicate that a teenager's level of self-esteem at age fifteen had either no relationship to, or a weak relationship to, substance dependence, mental health problems, life satisfaction, and relationship satisfaction. The environment the people were raised in played a more significant role and had a more lasting effect.

Depression and Suicidal feelings:

Do you, at times, feel sad, lost, or even confused? It is ok for many people to have such episodes. In most cases, it is a normal reaction to life's struggles, self-esteem issues or the loss of a loved one.

However, depression is another case. It can be associated with intense sadness and hopelessness. When it hinders you from your day-to-day activities and lasts for several days or weeks, it is worth talking to your doctor or seeking medical advice. There are several ways of trying to understand if a person has depression.

The following are some of the symptoms that manifest in someone who is going through depression:

•Fatigue on almost a daily basis or loss of the will to move.

•A sombre mood that starts in the morning and continues throughout the day.

•A feeling of guilt or worthlessness on an everyday basis

•Indecisiveness, impaired concentration

•The sense of being slowed down or restless.

•Significant weight gain or weight loss

•Hypersonic (oversleeping) or insomnia (lack of sleep) can manifest throughout the day nearing recurring suicide or death thoughts.

When someone has feelings such as a loss of interest in everything, they stop doing all the activities they were happily doing before, it might be a sign of depression. The symptoms above also happen to ordinary people and may not indicate depression, but they are more prevalent in people who are suffering from depression.

They will feel depressed daily or almost daily, and these feelings could last for a minimum of two weeks. These symptoms should not be the effect of medication or drugs for a diagnosis of depression. Feeling depressed or sad can be a normal reaction to life struggles, loss, or an injured self-esteem. This is our brain telling us that there is something wrong.

But suppose the brain keeps telling you that there is something wrong while objectively there is not anything wrong. In that case, it may mean that you are suffering from clinical depression, a severe but also very treatable medical condition.

Summary of what is depression in a single sentence: *"Depression is a feeling of intense sadness, worthlessness, hopelessness or helplessness that may last for more than days, weeks and sometimes months."* Approximately five in 100 adults have some form of depression annually. Sometimes it will last for just a couple of weeks. However, one in four women and one in ten men will get an episode of depression severe enough to require treatment.

Major Depression:

This type of depression is one, which does not last too long; it lasts between one to two weeks. If you experience this depression, you will feel terrible or sad a couple of times, but it does go away for a few weeks. Symptoms of major depression are loss of interest in life, suicidal thoughts, feeling guilty for no reason, weight loss or gain, sleeping less or too much, being tired all the time or having trouble concentrating. If one has low self-esteem, then they are at high risk of getting major depression.

Persistent Depressive Disorder (Dysthymia):

It has the same symptoms as major depression, but the person experiences it for two years or more. This is a more persistent version of major depression. It is very difficult for an individual to report this type of depression; this is because the symptoms become strong habits, and the individual tends to think "they always weren't like this". Also, it is more difficult for those around the sufferer to recognise if the individual has this type of depression. Those who are around the individual will think that this is the nature of their personality.

Irrespective of how you look at it, if someone struggles with negative thoughts or they are constantly in a negative mood, for longer than two weeks, you can almost certainly say that the individual is suffering from depression. If you ever felt down after an especially tiring day, cry after a bad breakup, or feel utterly miserable after being sacked from your job, that is a normal emotive reaction to have after an unpleasant situation or event. It is part of being, or what makes us human; however, when you feel unhappy for extended periods, weeks instead of hours and there seems to be no real reason for this sadness, you may be experiencing major depressive disorder or clinical depression.

How common is depression?

According to research, by 2025, depression will be the second biggest problem next to chronic heart disease when it comes to disability causes around the world. Statistics show that over 3 million people suffer from depression in the United Kingdom. Suicidal tendencies are also very high in people with this problem. Unfortunately, most adults who have clinical depression do not want to seek medical treatment. If left untreated, depression could result in greater suffering or even suicide.

Symptoms of all types of depression:

There is a range of depressive disorders, below is a list of those different types and their related symptoms:

Major Depressive Disorder (Major Depression):

Major depressive disorder or clinical depression is an illness that can affect a person emotionally, socially, and physically.

Symptoms of this depressive state are:

• You feel constantly sad or unhappy without any respite.

• A loss of appetite

• The inability to feel anything other than sadness, for example, not being able to feel excited about coming events, such as a birthday or even a wedding.

• Feeling empty or drained of everything.

- A feeling of hopelessness and helplessness, your future looks bleak and dark; there is not a speck of brightness on the horizon.

- Happiness is now met with dis-interest.

- A loss of energy, you are constantly feeling tired or lethargic. You may wake up tired even after a good night's sleep.

- Weight loss or gain

- Activities that used to bring you immense pleasure or happiness are now met with disinterest.

- Wishing you could fall asleep all the time or not at all.

- Lack of interest in sex

- Suicidal thoughts

- Low self-esteem or having a feeling that you are worthless.

Finally, if you ever feel like you wish to end your life, seek help immediately.

Dysthymia:

This is a form of depression that has overall mild symptoms, but these symptoms are chronic, as they can last for years. Symptoms of this chronic state of mood are:

- Daily activities will hold no interest to you, so you will feel demotivated to do them.

- Sadness

- Hopelessness

- A lack of energy

- Being hypercritical of yourself

- Quick to anger. You may frequently be snappy towards friends and family.

- Obsessing about your past actions

- Difficulties with sleeping

- Being described as a gloomy and pessimistic person will be a frequent occurrence in your life.

These symptoms will stay with the person for years but will fluctuate in intensity over this time. So, you may have good and bad days. Although it's normal to have good and bad days for most individuals, with Dysthymia, bad days will last for months at a time with only a few good ones thrown in once in a while.

Psychotic Depression:

This is a type of depression that is characterised by some form of a psychotic element. This means that alongside the classic depression symptoms, a person suffering from psychotic depression may experience hallucinations such as hearing voices or misconceptions of the reality of a situation, for example, the idea that you are worthless or sinful.

Postnatal depression:

This is a type of depression that mothers experience after giving birth. This change in mood can begin anytime during the first year after childbirth. It has been shown that around 10 to 15% of all new mothers will experience some form of postnatal depression, which can interfere with the raising of the child. The symptoms of this depressive disorder are:

•A loss of appetite

•Resentment or hatred towards the baby

•Loss of sex drive

•A feeling of inadequacy

•An inability to connect or bond with your child.

•Mood swings

•Inability to sleep.

•Withdrawing from your husband, family, and friends

•Thoughts of harming a child.

Seasonal Affective Disorder (SAD):

So, a person who feels blue during the long winter months may be experiencing SAD.

This form of depressive mood, which is triggered by the seasons, is classified as a seasonal affective disorder. The specific symptoms experienced are dependent on the season which gets you down.

Winter
- A feeling of heaviness

- Sleeping more often than usual

- Weight gain and cravings for fatty foods

- Irritability

- Not being friendly with people during the winter months. So, you may be extra snappy or irritable towards family, friends, or even strangers.

Summer
- Weight loss or gain

- Loss of appetite

- Inability to sleep.

- Anxiety

- Sadness

Bipolar disorder or manic-depressive disorder:

A person suffering from bipolar may feel euphoric one moment, and the next they can be extremely unhappy. A series of swings in emotions mark bipolar.

Symptoms of high mood:
- They will experience extreme happiness, to the extent of euphoria.

- Fast speech

- Poor decision-making skills

- Quick to anger.

- Irritability

- An increase in high-risk activity. Such activity includes unwise sexual habits, drinking too much or driving recklessly.

- A heightened interest in sex

- Carelessness in spending money

- Lack of enough sleep

Symptoms of low mood:
- Unhappiness

- A feeling of bleakness about the future

- Loss of sex drive

- Anxiety

•There will be a lack of pleasure in life.

•Loss of energy

Childhood Depression:

It can be just an everyday emotion while you develop. When you are sad, it does not necessarily mean that you are depressed. However, if you are persistently depressed daily, you might have an issue. Another symptom is that emotion disrupts your day-to-day activities, including schoolwork, family life and interests.

Teen Depression:

You are advised to speak to a doctor when you notice that you may be depressed for two consecutive weeks. You might be feeling introverted and not wanting to communicate. You can also feel secluded, and minimize contact with your friends. There are effective treatments that you can have to move on from depression. According to statistics, 1 in 8 teenagers suffers from depression. Depression in people is a serious matter that needs to be addressed promptly and properly.

Double Depression:

This happens when a person who is already inflicted with chronic depression experiences trauma, which leads to major depression. It is usually a condition found in people with long term as well as mild to moderate depression (dysthymia). These individuals tend to cycle between mild to moderate levels of dysthymia and deep low levels of major depression.

Secondary Depression:

This type of depression roots in a known medical condition such as Parkinson's disease, stroke, AIDS, or hypothyroidism. It can also come from psychiatric problems such as panic disorder, bulimia, or schizophrenia. It occurs in individuals who have one or more pre-existing, non-effective psychiatric disorders or an incapacitating or life-threatening medical illness that precedes and parallels the symptoms of depression.

Treatment-resistant Depression:

This type of depression might be chronic or long-lasting. This is a condition that does not respond well to treatments such as antidepressant pills. Some suggest that electroconvulsive therapy (ECT) is the way to go depending on the severity and nature of the depression.

Masked Depression:

This type of depression hides behind the physical complaints of a person where no cause can be pointed out. When people suffer from major depressive disorders, certain symptoms such as feelings of hopelessness, worthlessness, helplessness or low mood, anhedonia, lack of motivation, cognitive symptoms like difficulty concentrating and slow processing of information. If someone is suffering from masked depression these symptoms are not visible.

Some identifiers of masked depression include:

•Anger and irritability

•Extreme fatigue due to any identified organic disorder

•Extreme negative response to perceived or real criticism or rejection

•Difficulty concentrating, making major decisions, and remembering things.

•Lack of motivation and interest in previously found pleasurable activities.

•Headaches, backaches, stomach aches, musculoskeletal aches

Causes of Depression:

Several factors can contribute to the development of depression. It is usually not caused by one single event but by a combination of collective outcomes due to several events, personal factors other long-term elements. According to studies, continuing difficulties such as being in an abusive relationship, long time unemployment, extended exposure to work-related stress, or long-term loneliness tend to cause depression more often than recent life events.

However, recent negative events or a combination of these events with other factors can trigger depression in individuals who are already on the edge. Some of the contributing factors for depression include the following:

Personality

Some people have a higher risk of suffering from depression because they are perfectionists, worry a lot, lack self-worth, are pessimists, or are sensitive to criticism.

Family history

People with a family history of depression in their families are at high risk of experiencing depression. However, if you have a parent or a close relative with depression, it does not automatically make you depressed. Several other personal factors or circumstances are likely to determine whether you will experience depression or not.

Drug and Alcohol Abuse

Many depressed people also deal with drug or alcohol problems.

Serious medical illnesses

Medical illnesses can cause depression directly or triggered through stress and worry, mainly if the condition entails chronic pain all long-term management.

Conflict

Depression among biologically vulnerable people is often caused by personal conflicts or fights with family members or friends.

Certain Medications

There are drugs such as corticosteroids, the antiviral drug interferon - Alpha, and Accutane which may increase a person's risk of depression.

Loss or death of a loved one

Overwhelming grief or sadness over the death of a loved one may add up to a person's risk of being depressed.

Major events

Graduating, getting a new job, or even getting married may cause depression; so, can losing a job, moving to a new house, retiring, or getting divorced. These are events that might be difficult to handle for some, especially because they also bring about major changes.

Other Personal Problems

Mental illnesses, social isolation or being an outcast may trigger depression. Although depression is very common, it is usually misdiagnosed or ignored. However, leaving it untreated can lead to life-threatening situations, especially considering severe depression is associated with a high suicide rate.

Awareness and early diagnosis can help you overcome, or find qualified help. Once you notice that you or any of your loved ones show symptoms of depression, ask for help right away.

Treating Depression:

Once you have acknowledged that you indeed have depression, the next step you need to take is to find ways to alleviate the gloom. You can take three different paths on your journey to treat your depression, i.e., medication, therapy, or lifestyle changes.

Medication

We will cover this first, as many associate depression immediately with anti-depressants, however, you should always initially speak to a professional, and discuss if medication is necessary, or if you can overcome your depression by one of the other means, like lifestyle changes or natural solutions.

Antidepressants can help relieve the symptoms of clinical depression, seasonal affective disorder (SAD), and dysthymia. There are a few different types of antidepressants available that can aid in easing the symptoms of depression. The most common class of medication prescribed are selective serotonin reuptake inhibitors or SSRIs.

They increase the serotonin level and noradrenaline in the body, preventing your blood from absorbing some of the serotonin from your brain. Typical classes of antidepressants used for patients nowadays are Citalopram, Paroxetine, Zoloft, Lexapro, Prozac, Cymbalta, Venlafaxine and Luvox.

It is important to remember that a couple of adverse side effects may be experienced by a person while taking antidepressants. These include:

- Nausea

- Fatigue

- A loss of interest in sex

- Increased anxiety

- Restlessness

- Dizziness

- Weight gain

- Dry mouth

- Changes in bowel movements

- Headaches

- Excessive sweating

- Increased suicidal thoughts.

Most of these side effects should ease after the first three weeks of starting antidepressants. Antidepressants are far from being addictive, but there can be issues if you suddenly stop taking them. To cease taking this type of drug, you will need to discuss it thoroughly with a medical professional. Your doctor will formulate a safe plan to wean you off slowly and gradually so minimal side effects occur. If you suddenly stop taking antidepressants a whole host of unpleasant side effects can happen. These being:

•Nausea

•Headaches

•Anxiety

•Vomiting

•Extreme mood swings

•Insomnia

•Quick to rise to anger.

•Loss of coordination

•Brain shocks - weird sensations where it feels as if your brain is being shocked. Sometimes these shocks can be felt in other parts of your body. For psychosis depression, some people can be supported at home by friends or relatives, in addition to regular support from a skilled mental health professional.

However, at some point, hospitalisation may be necessary. It might happen in cases where the person is at risk of harming themselves or others. Hospitalisation would provide a safe environment where the patient can receive proper care and support, alongside health professionals who have a deeper understanding of the best way to treat them.

Drugs vs Natural Relief:

Like any other disease of the mind and psyche, depression can be treated in a variety of ways. In the 19th century, coinciding with medical breakthroughs and the economic advances of the time, ideas on how to combat depression took centre stage. Many blamed the industrial revolution, with its factories and workshops, for creating an atmosphere that made people feel alienated and insignificant. Still, scientists believe that certain biological processes and factors in the physical world influence the onset of depression. Today, however, experts are utilising both natural and synthetic ways on how to better treat depression. Let us weigh in on the two options:

Drugs as a way of treating depression:

Your nearby pharmacy may have a wide array of drugs designed specifically for the treatment of depression. Indeed, modern innovations have helped produce medication that helps in alleviating such psychological maladies. Antidepressants are available in numerous drug stores; however, specific types of these drugs are heavily regulated owing to the significant psychophysical changes they produce. Tricyclic antidepressants are often the most effective.

These drugs have the function of affecting two chemical messengers that influence depression, namely serotonin and norepinephrine. Selective serotonin reuptake inhibitors, on the other hand, are also widely prescribed by doctors.

These types of antidepressants are known to be safe and are tolerated by most people. For most people having trouble sleeping, reversible inhibitors of monoamine oxidase are usually taken as substitutes for other types of antidepressants since they are known to have fewer side effects. However, concerning influencing the number of neurotransmitters that motivate depression, these are considered far less effective.

Newer types of antidepressants have penetrated most pharmacies. Noradrenaline- serotonin specific antidepressants can be easily purchased anywhere. The minimal side effects they promise are no reason to defend these drugs. Weight gain and changes in one's sexual appetite can be some of their adverse effects. All these drugs have been proven to be effective in alleviating depression. However, you still need advice from your doctor to make the way clear towards using these drugs, and we can also assume they are not wallet-friendly.

Natural ways of coping with depression and anxiety

With consistent medication, you may as well tread the natural path to curing your depression. Bear in mind that although they are known to be effective, drugs can also irritate certain areas of your lifestyle and dependence can be the least of your problems. Your best bet usually is to ground your cure on an emotional level; anything that you feel can give you comfort.

Natural alternatives come in such activities as discovering a new hobby or having a little chat with someone closest to you. People have ways to cope with sadness, and it all depends on whether you want salvation from this melancholic pit or not. But not everyone can say that undergoing depression is an easy ride. Below are some natural remedies that can surely help you find your calm and beat the blues:

•Having a drink of hot chamomile tea can help you with relaxation and improve sleep. The flavonoids will help you induce relaxation.

•Daily meditation can help improve signs of depression; taking just 15 minutes to calm your mind and practising simple breathing techniques can do wonders to help, prevent, cope and manage your anxieties and depression.

•How about releasing your feeling of anxiety and depression by getting back to nature? Spend some time outside and take in some fresh air and sunlight; it will do you a lot of good and improve your mood and help you release any anxious feelings that you might be having.

•Eat a well-balanced meal and give your body and mind the energy you need to face the day. Eating healthy will improve your overall mood.

•Give your Vitamin B intake a boost. Vitamin B will stimulate your brain to produce more epinephrine, dopamine, and serotonin, all of which will improve your mood. Eating foods such as fish, cheese, spinach, bell peppers, shellfish etc., These contain high amounts of vitamin B.

•Improve yourself mentally and physically by exercising regularly. Regular exercise will release endorphins which will put you in a happy and good mood.

Chapter 4 - Stop and Think! Why are you sad?

Many people undergoing depression are not entirely sure how they ended up being sad. Others would deny themselves the reason or the basis of their sadness until they begin to tolerate their depression. We have understood that the motivators behind depression can take the form of physical and emotional factors. To take a materialistic view of things, it could be that the chemical interaction within your body influences moods and processes, but this has yet to be verified within medical academic circles. With that in mind, we can only return to the one thing for clarity, that is the individual.

What is bothering you?

People usually say they are confronted by sudden thoughts or memories that remind them of traumatic experiences or life events deemed significant in a negative light. Studies have shown that nearly all people suffering from depression have no clear idea of why they are suffering in the first place, adding to the intrigue of the human mind. But if we are to tap into certain facets of patients' thoughts, whims, and desires, we might be able to come close to tapping into the root of their depression and determine the ultimate cure for it.

Using conversation as a cure:

This method is simple; If you are undergoing depression, you are usually interrogated or put on a spot by a clinical psychologist. However, it has been a trend that most patients would rather not tell their honest opinions about themselves; in some cases, they might be trying to mislead their interviewers with hazy answers and exaggerated anecdotes. Most people would choose to deny expressing themselves.

It is more likely that they feel that none of their depression will remain incurable for an indefinite amount of time, or they are so melancholic about it that any attempts towards social interaction are taboo. Yes, it can be a gruelling task sometimes. However, this method helps you to clear thoughts of anything that may contribute to these morose feelings of uselessness and distrust. Your therapist instead is there to aid you in this process, and you can only trust that sharing what you are really feeling, being honest with them and not holding back will gradually lift the burden of sadness from you.

Psychologist Vs Psychiatrist

Clinical psychologists will be highly trained in the diagnosis of mental, emotional, and behavioural illnesses. They do not prescribe medications but instead use psychological techniques such as psychoanalytic therapy and cognitive behaviour therapy. On the other hand, psychiatrists are medical doctors who can prescribe medications, and they are likely to look first at any medical factors behind whatever mental problems you might be experiencing. In most cases, someone with a mental illness might see both a psychiatrist and a psychologist to receive therapy and medication.

Expression is key

Being depressed does not give you a reason to stay reclusive. But, on a positive note, you can use your reclusiveness to your advantage. It gives you the leeway to judge certain facets of your life and examine which of these aspects bother you most. Could it be that people have become too shallow for you?

Were there any events in your past that put you in your current situation today? Try to be honest with yourself. Your depression did not come out of the blue, or we cannot just assume that it resulted from the reactions of certain hormones in your body. Perhaps, certain aspects of your life need careful reflection; you will achieve real answers when you can start confronting your life's realms.

Therapy or Counselling:

Therapy or Counselling is a form of treatment that can be done alongside medication or by itself; it involves discussing issues or concerns which make you feel unhappy. The crucial thing you need to decide concerning this form of treatment is the person you will be talking to about your depression. To accomplish this, first, ask your doctor for a list of recommended therapists or counsellors. Next, make appointments with several of the names which appear on the list.

Meet with them to see what you think of them. Do they make you feel comfortable? Or perhaps the opposite, do they make you feel awkward and uncomfortable? Furthermore, look at the space where the therapy will take place. Is it comforting and warm or sterile and cold? Find a location and person that will make for the most supportive environment. If this means meeting with several people until you find the perfect one, then so be it. Therapy is about you and trying to rid of the debilitating sadness you have found yourself trapped within.

Therapy can be beneficial in alleviating depression for several reasons. It can be incredibly therapeutic talking through issues in your life that have caused grief or stress, such as divorce or death in the family. Therapy can also provide strategies to cope with depression; it can help you change specific thought patterns or behaviour; for example, learning not to be so harshly critical of yourself.

Seek help or Talk to Someone!

We have previously noted that seeking help from friends and loved ones can help you overcome depression. Social relations have functions that go beyond utility. Sure, we can depend on our parents or friends for certain things like money or favours.

But it is the emotional attachment of these relations that defines the human experience. And indeed, having known you for a long time, your friends and family can serve as emotional walls for you to lean on when sadness gets the better of you. To do this, you must first acknowledge the need to overcome social anxiety. Communication is vital and a fundamental human need, and you certainly need to exercise it to confront your emotions.

Friendly Advice

Your friends can serve very well, the purpose of being your trusty confidants. You have known each other for ages, gone from hell and back, forging sisterly or brotherly solidarity. And you would not hesitate to give each other advice on just about anything. If the going gets tough as your depression progresses, the best thing to do is ask for a lending hand from your friends. They know you quite well, and it would strike them as odd when they see you depressed, given that they have not witnessed you feeling this way before. Be open to your friends about what you feel. It could be that your depression may have been caused by a sense of alienation or simply a feeling that you are always left out. Your friends may provide you with helpful advice as they are now acquainted with the way you view things.

Familial Advice

Next to friends, your family may also have an idea on how best to remedy your sense of loneliness. Since they have witnessed how you have grown over time, your parents could invoke wisdom in solving your problems, whatever forms they take. Your parents, having the role of protectors, would also feel empathy towards you. You might have had a rough time at school or work; you might have been devastated by a recent divorce or break-up.

In such instances, you need to gain clarity, something that can shed a rational light on your situation. And by adding their own experiences to the dialogue, your parents can provide you with the knowledge on how best to confront emotional blockades. Try to open up to your siblings too. They may as well be concerned with what their brother or sister is going through.

Expert Advice

Still, you can always consult experts in the study of human emotions and the psychological and biological forces at work. Contact your doctor or local psychiatrist; it may involve a large amount of money to pay for the sessions and the prescribed medication, but it can help in the long term, mainly when the depression is deeply rooted in the psyche.

Chapter 5 - Effects of Depression

Physical:

Depression influences one's physical well-being.

Here are several physical effects of depression:

- 2 out of 3 people experience aches and pains.
- Daily fatigue
- Decreased libido.
- Lack of sleep, insomnia, or oversleeping at times.

The lack of a chemical in your body called serotonin happens when the brain wires differently. People who have chronic depression are sensitive to increased pain. Many of them complain of back pain. Serotonin also has an impact on the sex lives of depressed individuals.

Depression can cause problems in relationships. Sadly, for many people with depression, their doctors and families overlook the signs. There is a case where people were found fatigued, with insomnia and were dismissed as just ageing but, they were depressed. Some assumed that depression was an inevitable part of growing old. The elderly who are lonely and isolated are at most risk of miss diagnosis. Common triggers of depression later on in life might include things such as losing the ability to drive, facing changing health, moving or even coping with unexpected deaths of grandchildren and children.

Physical illness and depression:

When you are stressed, cortisol rises, which increases your risk for several diseases. It can affect your body by targeting your immune system. When this happens, you will not be able to fend off infection. Even if you are vaccinated, its effect is not that strong anymore. There is also a report that depression leads people to drug or alcohol abuse.

Medical Illness and Depression:

Physical challenges that have been brought upon the person suffering from depression are said to weaken their immune system. In effect, existing illnesses might get worse. Physical changes that are caused by depression or illness might trigger or make the depression chronic. Serious illnesses that are associated with depression are:

- Stroke

- Heart Attack

- Coronary Artery Disease

- Lupus or multiple sclerosis

- Parkinson's disease

- Cancer

- HIV/AIDS

- Arthritis
- Diabetes
- Kidney disease

Ways to Beat Anxiety:

Anxiety spells trouble and, in some cases, a tragedy for people who cannot control it. The anticipation of the future makes one nervous but is not necessarily found on a basis. Cranky people are usually anxious about their day-to-day activities. They experience poor concentration, sleeping problems, or just plainly distressed. There are simple ways to escape stress. Here are just some of them:

- **De-clutter your mind**

Escape stress by organizing your workspace. Wherever you are going to stay for numerous hours, tidy up. Regularly cleaning your workspace or home makes things easy for your mind. It will also get your blood flowing.

- **Show Gratitude**

Studies have shown that expressing gratitude to someone reduces anxiety. You can start by creating a journal and writing about the people you want to thank and appreciate.

- **Eat Right**

Anxious people do not usually eat the correct type of food. Eat foods that have omega-3 and Vitamin B. You can add whole grain carbohydrates to the mix. Eating healthy will help your body cope with stress in the workplace or school. Eating sugar does not help at all, even if your body is telling you to indulge.

- **Breathe Properly**

When you experience panic attacks, breathe. Inhale, exhale; Repeat until you calm down. Take long, deep breaths to decrease the possibility of increasing your anxiety levels. When you consciously breathe, it will signal to your brain that it needs to calm down.

- **Meditate**

Research shows that by meditating, grey matter increases in the brain. It teaches the body how to relax. Meditation also helps us to analyse how our body works and its trigger points. Also, there are positive effects of meditation, such as a decrease in anxiety attacks, improving mood and elimination of some stress symptoms. Meditation is excellent for people who want to relax and exercise their minds. Deep breathing or a mantra of positive thoughts helps a person calm down and de-stress.

Originated in the Buddhist tradition, meditation is for spiritual enlightenment. Meditation can also definitely help a depressed person sleep better by incorporating breathing techniques. Meditation lowers stress and anxiety. It also improves your confidence, relationships, self-acceptance, creativity, and concentration.

Your meditation session only needs to last for 5 minutes to see instant results. Meditation allows you to live within the moment and gives you respite from all your worries, fears, phobias, and negative thoughts. Meditate for 20 minutes daily for maximum results. Allow yourself to relax in a quiet place, focus on your breathing and let all thoughts waver by.

• **Make a Vision Board**

Creating a vision board helps you feel optimistic about the things that lie ahead; Setting goals and seeing the results can take anxiety off your shoulder. This board will help you get moving towards your goals and projects. Do not marry your work! Go out and have fun occasionally. Do things that will help you escape the stress. Create your playtime by engaging in activities such as sports, singing, dancing, hanging out with your friends or playing.

• **Silence**

Even for just 5 minutes, be silent and disconnect from the world. Do not answer emails, TV or the telephone; Noise can put your stress levels up. Quiet times will do wonders for your overall mental health.

• **Smile**

Smiling is not rocket science. Anyone can do it; If you are stressed out with work, it is best to read something online or talk to a co-worker about things that make you giggle. Psychologists at the University of Kansas found that the idea of smiling decreases the effects of depression, so try watching something funny on Netflix or listening to a funny podcast, it will help move your focus and relax your brain.

A mindset to beat depression!

Depression is a serious problem. Many people think that their problems cannot be fixed at all. Others turn to unsafe medications when they feel down, and it is never safe for them. Changing one's mindset is one way to go when you feel you are up against a brick wall. People who are depressed feel like they are useless, and their lives are full of suffering. They want to deal with the problem, but the realities are proving too much to handle. One thing that proves to work most of the time is analysing the problem and dealing with it.

Yoga is one good way of moving your body effortlessly. Once you get your body moving, your mind will follow; Yoga also helps alleviate your stress. When you clear your mind, you get to think about your situation and the things that you do about it. Sadness is a normal emotion, and so are feelings of melancholy, anger, and mourning. To be truly happy, you must embrace these feelings. Approaching these feelings with a growth mindset is good for your mind and soul. Here are some things that can help you shift away from depression:

Help yourself through questioning, here are some of those questions you might want to consider:

What can I do to change the way I think?

What am I grateful for today?

Where will I be in 5 years if I continue doing the same things I am doing now?

Am I who I want to be?

How long has it been since I committed a random act of kindness? Is my outlook on life an optimistic or pessimistic one?

Do I wake up every day with hope and excitement? Do I worry too much?

Some of the above questions might help you grow and realise what needs to change. Think about yourself, and how you interact with other people. Having such thoughts might reveal something that will surprise you for the better. Start something for yourself; do something that will make you feel good. You can turn to arts and crafts.

You can write a poem, a book, start gardening or finish that treehouse that has been sitting in the backyard for years. Let your soul express itself. Change your actions! It is always beneficial to move your body rather than stay in the house and pity yourself. Open your soul and heart to new adventures. Release the sadness and let in your good energy. Appreciate all the feelings that you are experiencing and let them out. Cry if you want to or break a cheap plate if you feel the need to vent your anger on something. Accept and see the goodness in your sadness. Acknowledging your feelings can sometimes be liberating.

Chapter 6 - Setbacks, suicide and how to get help!

Depression is a difficult obstacle to overcome. The road to recovery is rifled with drawbacks which can put a snag in your process of booting the blues. There are a few traps that a person may fall into, and these will hinder your recovery from depression.

These include:

Do not let negative thoughts overrun you.

While depressed, negative thoughts can quickly overwhelm a person. Dark and bleak thoughts will occupy the mind, things like "I am a failure", "I am such a loser", "No one likes me", and "I am just a burden". These types of thoughts will bombard a depressed person constantly. It might seem like there is little hope for respite from them. It is best that you stop and rationally think through these negative emotions.

It is important to remember that this is your warped point of view shining through, and it is far from the reality of the situation. Repeat a positive mantra when you are feeling especially down about yourself. This could be something like "I am a valid, important person; I matter; my opinions matter. I am a brilliant, beautiful person." Repeat positive and uplifting thoughts in your head, your subconscious mind will start to believe this over time, and eventually, this will translate into better moods, a better self-image, and a higher quality of life.

Drinking: People reach for that glass of whiskey because they hope to find happiness in that amber liquid. But this is far from the reality of the situation. Yes, you may feel relaxed and happy while drinking those first few glasses; however, this mellow mood can evaporate quickly as the night goes on. Furthermore, regularly drinking can have significant negative impacts on brain chemistry.

Let it out: It is easy to keep all your sadness, anger, and resentment bottled up, but it is extremely unhealthy and will not benefit you in the long run. If you feel like it is getting a little too much and you feel awash with negative emotions, then the best course of action is to confide in a trusted individual. This could be your mum, dad, best friend, sister, brother, or therapist. This means anyone you can trust to be supportive and render a listening ear when you voice your emotions and issues.

Suicide

Sadly, people who suffer from depression have a high risk of attempting or committing suicide. Suicidal thoughts bombard a depressed person. Thoughts like, "I can finally rest and stop feeling so sad if I just killed myself", "everyone will be better off if I was not here", or "they will regret everything when I'm gone". If these thoughts get unbearable and you truly feel like you wish to end your life and have started planning how to accomplish it, stop and get immediate help. This can be accomplished in the form of seeking support and help from a loved one or by calling your local suicide helpline or the Samaritans. The world might look like a bleak wasteland from your current point of view, but this is your LIFE which you are contemplating extinguishing for good. Try to remember that this dark place you are presently living in is a temporary place, and there is a future out there with lots of potential laughs, smiles and happiness awaiting you.

Coping with suicidal thoughts:

Suicidal thoughts are feelings about hurting yourself or taking your own life. Suicide can be linked to depression. Suicidal views can happen to anyone – young and old, male or female for several reasons. People tend to have these thoughts when they are having intense emotional pain, and they do not see a way out. The issues that cause this type of pain will be different for everyone. Suicide often is preventable and avoidable. There are multiple risk factors for suicide – these include:

- Age, Gender, Poor physical and mental health, History of violence

- Family history of suicide, Having weapons at home, Recently been released from a long stay in jail or prison.

- Hanging out with others who talk about suicide or are encouraging you to take your own life.

Suicide warning signs

•Feeling trapped or hopeless. The sufferer feels like they need to escape

•A person feels unbearable emotional or physical pain

•The sufferer focuses on death, violence or dying

•They feel that friends and family would be better off without them.

•Making plans or searching for a way to take their life

•Feeling guilty or shame

•Using drugs and alcohol more frequently

•Withdrawing from friends and family – no longer have an interest in the things they enjoy

•Giving away things that mattered to them

•Writing a note, making a will or putting their affairs in order

A history of suicide increases the risk of future attempts on one's own life. If you know someone who has mentioned suicide, serious actions must be taken. If you are planning to take your own life, it is best to go to the hospital for treatment or speak to a trusted friend or family member straight away for support. You can even ask them to read this next section of this book, to help them understand how you are feeling and how they might be able to help you.

Supporting friends and family with depression and anxiety:

Supportive and good relationships are integral elements of the recovery process with depression. The person who is going through depression will occasionally look to you for help and may seek you out as a place to vent their emotions or share their concerns. It will be your job to be a non-judgemental ear where they can voice their feelings without any fear of censure or reprove. Avoid unhelpful and incredibly insensitive remarks such as "Harden up", or "stop being such a cry baby". Depression is not just the Blues or something you can easily shake off like a sprinkling of snow. Depression is a deep pit of despair that pulls the sufferer further and further in until darkness and desolation surround them. It is incredibly hard to claw yourself up from this overwhelming darkness. Below is a list of things you should and should not do concerning helping someone with depression:

What you should do:

Have Fun: This means spending quality time with your loved ones. This time does not have to be spent talking about their depression, but rather trying to concentrate on having a good time. Ask them whether they wish to do something; it could be taking a walk around a lake, going to an art exhibition, or catching a flick at the movies. This time should be relaxed and casual, with little stress and no expectations.

Opening your ears and closing your mouth: This situation is not about you, but them. This means try to let them do all the talking, and you can just lend a supportive ear. However, when you are prompted by them, you are more than welcome to give advice.

Support: Try to aid your loved ones in getting help, either in the form of a doctor's appointment or encouraging them to engage in lifestyle changes. This means when they go for a walk, ask if they want company, or you could make them a healthier fresh dinner.

What you should not do:

Dial it down a bit: The most important thing you have to remember when supporting someone with depression is not to push them. Let them come to you; do not pry or pester them with constant questions about their mood. Do not ask them constantly if they're feeling okay or if they're feeling better. There is a big difference between being there for someone and smothering them.

Tough love: Telling a depressed person to harden up or get over it is definitely not the best course of action. This is not something you can snap out of in a minute; depression is a serious illness with a long road to recovery. Also, do not spout clichés such as "Hey, come on! Think of all the people worse off than you!" or "It could be worse". This type of pep talk is not helpful.

I have to go: Do not avoid the person who is suffering. This will make them feel infinitely small about themselves and will not help with their depression.

Signs of possible feelings of suicide:

If your loved one is depressed or they are expressing suicidal thoughts, talk to them about it or call an expert. Do not wait for anything bad to happen; call someone who knows and can handle whatever your loved one is going through. Warning signals of suicide:

- Talking about suicide and wanting to do it
- Talking about harming others or harming oneself
- Impulsiveness or aggressive behaviour
- Making plans or researching different ways to die
- Displaying extreme changes in mood
- Sleeping or eating more or less
- Use of alcohol or drugs more often.
- Extreme sadness, anxiousness, signs of agitation and sometimes full of rage

- Complaints of unbearable emotional or physical pain

What happens if they do not want help?

Someone who is depressed or anxious may be reluctant to get help or talk about their feelings. It would be largely up to you, the friend or family member, to coax them into accepting the fact that they have a problem and need help. If they at anytime voice a desire to kill themselves, get them immediate help even if it's unwanted.

Chapter 7 - 28 Lifestyle changes to combat depression and anxiety!

Feeling low is not easy for anyone. Apart from eating healthy foods and changing your mindset, there are certain things that you need to change with your lifestyle if you wish to combat depression.

Exercise

Be it going to the gym and working out for half an hour or doing a 30-minute walk; exercise can improve your mood tremendously. Exercise produces hormones to combat depression. It is a natural antidepressant.

Studies have revealed that 30 minutes a day for up to four months of exercise helped people with depression by improving their mood, reducing stress and anxiety, providing a great night's sleep and boosting self-esteem. Physical activity stimulates brain chemicals that promote relaxation euphoria—exercise bands off the tension that leads to depression. You will be in a better physical shape and feel good about your appearance when you exercise; this boosts your confidence.

So, put on your running shoes, neon spandex dancing gear, all your flashy swimsuits and get out there, be active. Being active for only 20 to 30 minutes a day can have a significant improvement in your mood. It is because exercise boosts your serotonin levels as well as releases endorphins.

Exercise is an easy and inexpensive way to try and cast away the gloom. Try to mix up your exercises so that monotony does not arise. The least you want is for the exercise, which is supposed to make you happy, to become a tedious chore you dread. So, trek through beautiful mountains one sunny Saturday, swim laps on a Tuesday and go for a run-on Thursday. Mix it up and have fun.

Psychological benefits of exercise

When you exercise, the endorphins released in your body reduce pain; they also trigger a good feeling in your body. It can be related to morphine; after a quick run, many people feel "euphoric", or another word for it is "runners high", leading to a more positive outlook on life.

Endorphins are natural analgesics because they diminish the feeling of pain. They reside in a person's spinal cord, brain and other parts of your body where neurotransmitters exist. The neuroreceptors where endorphins bind are the same ones that pain medicines bind to; one good thing about endorphins is that they are not addictive like morphine.

Other benefits of regular exercise:

•Boost Self-esteem

•Reduce stress.

- It pushes depression and anxiety away.
- Lowers blood pressure.
- Strengthens your heart.
- Increases energy levels.
- Builds the strength of bones.
- Improves muscle tone and strength.
- Reduces body fat.
- It makes you healthy and fit.

Exercise is not often used as a treatment for moderate depression. Certain types of exercise are more helpful for people with depression; these include :

- Dancing
- Biking
- Golf
- Gardening
- Jogging
- Housework
- Aerobics
- Walking

- Swimming

- Yoga

Joining group classes might be beneficial for people with depression because of the much-needed support and sometimes the interaction. You can also exercise with your friends; doing group exercises will give you emotional comfort when you know that others are supporting you. If you have always been moving, joining exercise classes will be straightforward. However, if you are not active and you are over 50 years old, or you have some kind of medical condition, it is best to talk to your doctor first before starting an exercise programme.

Wondering how often you need to exercise to alleviate the symptoms of depression? To get the endorphins going, it takes at least 30 minutes of exercise, three times a week. If you have a lot of time, exercising more is better. If you're just starting, it is wise to take it easy. Before you start an exercise programme, think first about an easy routine that you can maintain and follow. It can be dancing, running, or whatever you enjoy doing, just as long as you are comfortable with the activity and the time that you are giving it. If you are going to start as soon as possible, try to incorporate it into your daily routine. Schedule it and put it on the things to do for the day; Variety is important.

Try to mix and match and find people that you can work out with, do not spend a lot of money on exercise programmes; however, if you choose to join a gym, canvas first before buying any membership.

Weight Loss

Losing weight can improve your health and self-esteem. It also gives your mind some needed clarity. You do not have to drastically drop your weight; you can eat right and exercise daily. Avoid hoping onto fad diets. It will not do you any good, and chances are, the weight that you will lose is not permanent. You are guaranteed to put back all the lost weight when you resume your normal eating habits. Do not go for fad diets where you need to eat certain juices or types of food for a week to drop weight. You need to eat foods that are nutritious to calm you down.

Sleep

Feeling fatigued from sleep deprivation can heighten depression symptoms and increase anxiety. Sufferers have a hard time sleeping. Lying awake at night is hard, especially when your brain does not want to calm down. There can also be times when you wake up for no reason at all and cannot get back to sleep afterwards. To get some "shut-eye", make a bedtime routine that follows a sleep schedule. Change your sleep routine to a healthy good night's rest. Try to sleep 8-10 hours a day. Maximise the quality of your sleep by sleeping in a very dark room, turning off all electric devices, and by waking up without an alarm. Waking up without an alarm can be difficult at first, but this is a habit that you can train very easily. Try to sleep 8-10 hours before you need to wake up; this will help you to wake up automatically.

Depression and Insomnia are related!

Depression has its roots in the neuro-physical processes of the body, and it can directly affect sleeping patterns. In fact, the main symptoms that defined depression include the inability to sleep or the lack thereof. People suffering from depression describe their ordeal as gruelling, especially when they are unable to sleep at night. Besides food and shelter from natural forces, sleep has been a fundamental aspect of human life as much as it is an important need for many other organisms. Our bodies need to recharge and rejuvenate themselves to maintain their fully functioning or daily existence.

Sleep enables our organs, especially the neurotransmitters in our brains, to get enough rest to replace worn-out cells. But it should not imply that the whole body is shutdown momentarily; it continues to function. Sleep merely limits physical energy and thus gives ample time for worn-out cells to rejuvenate. It does seem boring to go to sleep at the sensible time of 10:30 -11 pm, but a solid 7 8 hours of sleep a night can have a significant impact on your mood. If you stay up late glued to the Internet, then you will be crankier and irritable, and regarding the big picture, it will worsen your depression.

Hours of peaceful and calm sleep are essential to your plan of kicking depression in its clammy backside. Sleep is an important part of life. Lacking some well-earned sleep can have both emotional and biological consequences that are not far from being significant.

Lacking Sleep

Patients with depression find it difficult to shut their eyes at night, and they are usually kept awake by thoughts that instigate their low feelings. Some pointed out that they are hard-pressed at urging themselves to sleep, while others reported difficulty staying asleep. Consequently, some suffer from daytime sleepiness as a result of staying awake at night.

Especially when one has a stable career, it can be difficult to cope with trying to stay productive. Depressed people are not at their most effective when they suffer from an excruciating lack of sleep. The depression deepens when Insomnia has significantly taken over one's consciousness. Sufferers also say that with Insomnia comes paranoia. Not having the rest and time that is needed to replace worn-out cells, the mind will react to certain stimuli in peculiar ways. Insomniacs will find it hard to maintain a logical flow of thoughts, resulting in awkward conversations and the inability to socialise with colleagues.

Some sufferers can also get easily irritated by the subtlest things, will come across as rude and will often be misunderstood by other people in the workplace. On a biological note, sufferers are prone to fits of nausea; they may also feel limp and have sensations of discomfort in certain limbs.

Getting Sleep

As we have seen earlier, sleep is an indispensable part of everyday human life, and it can very well be a cure for some people's depression and anxiety. It is possible to be depressed or anxious while getting the right amount of sleep. However, sleep can form an apt remedy by allowing your mind to relax. Lack of enough sleep also can render you mindless and agitated by the thoughts that keep you awake. If you are indeed having sleeping problems, consult with your doctor, who may prescribe appropriate medication. Try to limit caffeine intake and eating a well-balanced diet can form part of the vital steps required to combat sleep deprivation.

Read Every Day

Studies show that if you just read for just half an hour a day, it will provide many positive benefits. Reading stimulates tranquillity and relaxation. When you read spiritual books, it can lower your blood pressure and make you relaxed. Reading self-help books helps people to deal with suffering and mood disorders. Reading books also improves mental stimulation and brain memory. When you read a book, you are exerting mental effort; this allows you to train your brain. The brain requires exercise to improve (just like a muscle). Other benefits of reading are stress reduction, knowledge improvement, vocabulary expansion, concentration improvement, better writing skills and improving analytical skills.

Don't Isolate Yourself.

When you surround yourself with people, you do not allow yourself to buy into all your negative thoughts. Talking to a trusted friend, support group, or family member can improve your mood and make you feel better about yourself. You need a supportive mastermind who lifts you up when you don't feel motivated to cope with your depression. Also, try to provide value when you are with people. Value can be provided in the form of positivity, someone who listens to others, helps people, or even a smile. Providing value helps to remove pressure and focus from yourself.

The common mistake that most people undergoing depression make is to cut off ties with the world. I do not mean trying to isolate oneself from society, particularly one you entirely depend on, but I am referring to an attempt at avoiding any social contact with friends, family members or people who just want to help you go through the sadness.

Depressed people make it a reason for their condition that the world has decided to turn on them; that it cannot be controlled no matter how firmly they set their minds to it. Sufferers do not acknowledge the fact that the world acts in unfathomable ways. We cannot always get the grade or promotion we wanted or attract our childhood crush.

The universe revolves around probabilities, but sadly most of us try to deny such facts. Depressed people feel they are vulnerable, which explains their diminished amount of self-esteem and lack of motivation to do anything productive. And we can always assume that forging social relationships can be a productive endeavour. We need people as much as plants need the sun to survive.

By depriving yourself of any social interaction, you are trying to convince the world that you do not need friends or family to enjoy life. Some melancholic sufferers will go as far as pointing out that their friends and family contribute to their depression, but this is often just how it feels rather than fact.

Be Active

By allowing yourself to engage in mental and physical labour, you can gradually decrease the effects of depression. Being depressed forces you to sulk; sadness saps you of any significant amount of energy needed for productive and recreational work. Depression, to be concise, put you in a condition of feeling utterly useless.

You will eventually try to convince yourself that life, being dull and absurd, is not worth living; you will be trapped in some form of paradox. The longer you remain in an idle situation, the more you become melancholic, which in turn gives a perceived reason to remain idle. Furthermore, with an idle mind and faced with no other tasks at hand, engulfed by the depression, you will endure more suffering. The situation becomes worse over time until the sufferer declares they have had enough. Action is always a way to solve a problem!

Caring for your Career

A person who has a career can deem it difficult to carry out their duties and tasks in the workplace if they are depressed. Sadness tries to pull them down and de-motivates them from doing day-to-day tasks effectively. They are also forced to dislike any sort of contact with colleagues.

The worse this gets, their reputation within the working environment diminishes, and the possibility of earning more opportunities suffers. If you, indeed, feel that work has become lonesome and dull for you, then you may have to see it in a different light. Look to your career for an apt cure that can help you stand on your feet and become the life of the office again. You can do so by setting your mind on your daily tasks. Occupied by work, your mind can easily focus on other things and will begin to set aside thoughts that cause depression.

Exercise your mind

Try and engage in recreational and intellectual activities during your free time. Work cannot be the only thing you should depend on to counter the effects. Read books, solve crosswords or Sudoku puzzles or unless you are alone, strike up an interesting conversation with another person in the room. Doing any of these can help your mind off the things which make you sad as well as stimulate your cognitive faculties.

Hobbies Matter

There is also a need for you to engage in your favourite hobbies, especially those that are creative. Whether it is painting or writing songs, or composing poems, you can never go wrong with engaging in your creative passions. Through these, you can effectively express yourself in a way that suits you. Creative work also encourages you to liberate your mind from anything that gets you down in the dumps. It comes across as a form of therapy that lets you put your sadness on paper or canvas. Psychologists urge their patients to undertake creative activities; it is a tried and tested approach.

Try something new

Embrace risk by trying new things, and your mind might just acquire a reason to forget being depressed. If the depression is getting heavy with your current remedies, then you might as well try a different approach; Try new things. Do you always want to skydive or bungee jump? Maybe you have that itch to travel to a place you have yet to get acquainted with?

Avoid Negative friends

Negative friends tend to bring you down emotionally. When you are vulnerable to negative thoughts, a negative person can undo all the hard work you did to become and remain positive in a snap. When you hang out with negative people long enough, it does not matter how much willpower you have; your subconscious mind will grab and take over their mindsets.

This will result in you becoming very negative. So, the best way to deal with negative people is to avoid them and slowly remove them from your life. If the negative person is someone you cannot avoid, then there are other subtle techniques for dealing with them.

How to politely deal with negative people:

Firstly, do not engage with negativity.

It is quite easy to get drawn into the negativity of someone else. But do not engage; not engaging does not mean you simply ignore that person, but it means that you take your emotional distance from the person. When someone focuses on negative talk, choose to answer in a very short way. Again, you don't need to be rude. Answering short, nonchalant but at the same time positive is a perfect mix.

Be supportive.

Be willing to listen to the person with a compassionate ear and provide help if they ask for it (don't try to force your beliefs; this will seldom help). Sometimes someone just has a negative day or phase and needs help. If the person tends to continue their negativity with the same topic, then it is time to disengage from them.

Disarm their negativity with positivity.

The best way to disarm their negativity is to redirect the negative topics into positive ones. Do not be abrupt with it because that can look like you don't care about them. Be subtle and gently redirect the topic with something funny or a well-meant compliment.

Minimise the alone time between the two of you:

When you are hanging out with a negative person, try to hang out with them in groups. This will allow the negative person to take over the positivity of the whole group. And it is a lot easier for you because the person does not focus their negativity on you but on the whole group.

Set boundaries

Realise that their negativity is not your responsibility. If they still bring you down, it is time to avoid them as much as possible. If it is a colleague, cut them short. If it is a family member, try to spend time away from them, or you can even choose to refuse to answer their calls.

Reduce time spent on Social Media, TV, The News, Movies and Games:

Quite often, we compare ourselves to others when exposed to a lot of social media. These things overstimulate the brain. This leads to low self-esteem, sabotages you to avoid accomplishing your goals, and it can lead to more depression. TV overstimulates the brain and can trigger addictions and expose a sense of instant gratification. The news can trigger anxieties (and some news provide a lot of misleading news). Movies and video games are powerful emotional stimuli for either happiness or depression.

Alcohol

Drinking a lot of alcohol can make you depressed in the long term. This creates a vicious cycle of depression (due to alcoholism and binge drinking), leading to your inability to cope with depression. Alcohol is also linked to the habit of making bad decisions and being impulsive.

Smoking

Smoking constricts the blood vessels in the brain. This can trigger mental disorders; trying to quit smoking and binge smoking can reduce your mental health issues and increase your confidence.

Re-frame everything.

Reality is made in our minds, so the art is to re-frame everything into something positive. Many times, when we become depressed and are flooded with negative thoughts, this is because we address the ups and downs in our life in an improper way. What will tend to happen is that our subconscious mind will adopt these mindsets eventually, and we will become happier in the long run. For example, when you are having a bad day, you can either think, "I am having a bad day", "I am feeling down", or you can think: "Bad days are a part of the journey to becoming something bigger". So essentially, it is not a bad day!

List your accomplishments.

It is one thing to look at your past failures and reflect, but it is another to fixate and become too hard on yourself because of your past failures. We tend to give our past failures more "airtime" than our accomplishments. Start writing your accomplishments every day before going to bed. Your mind will process this in your sleep, and you will feel more positive every day.

Laugh and Smile More

You simply cannot have negative thoughts while smiling and laughing all day long. Physically smile and laugh more. The mind follows the body; Try and find everything funny, even the smallest things. Do you remember when you used to laugh about everything when you were little? It is the same thing. Or think about a baby who laughs about everything. Depression or negative thoughts are products of our environment. If you are a realist and don't like to "fake it", you can re-frame everything into something funny.

Set Daily Goals

Start your day by setting small goals that you can accomplish. When we are depressed, we tend to have low self-esteem. We can easily get more self-esteem by accomplishing goals. Pick five things that you want to achieve the next day. Make sure that these goals are small but challenging enough to go for.

For example, I want to achieve five things tomorrow: no consumption of processed sugar, going to the gym, giving five people an honest compliment, going to bed early, and calling my sister and saying that I love her. When you achieve those five small goals every day, you will get self-esteem. This is because you are providing proof for your brain that you actually can achieve everything you want.

Challenge Your Negative Thoughts

You need to challenge your thoughts and go all the way. Just stating that a specific thought is not true is not enough. Your brain is smart enough to realise that you are resisting a thought without a legitimate reason. Challenge them from logical and objective standpoints. So, for example, if your thought is: "I am worthless", continue by asking: "Why am I worthless?" A reason will pop up, and you need to challenge that reason again. What about all the people that would say you really provide value to them? And so on.

Make time for yourself. Go on holiday by yourself, read a book, go for a hike and do something that you really enjoy; find somewhere where you can really charge your mental battery. If you are depressed because you are constantly working or are having responsibilities without ever having time to chill, you need to take a little time off. But if you are someone who is always locked up, I encourage you to take a little time off. If you spend time with your family, go and socialise with people or do something else where you are getting in touch with positive people.

Stop Criticising yourself

We all have the image in our heads of the person that we need to be right now. This is a sense of a positive mindset, but also a very negative one. We are holding standards for ourselves and want more out of life, but, at the same time, it can occur that we do not appreciate what we have, whom we have in our lives, and what strengths we possess. This can discourage us and give us the feeling of being worthless. If you want to improve yourself, you should be honest about your flaws but let them go at the same time. Acknowledge your flaws, work hard every day to improve, and do not think about the flaws that you have at the moment. Besides, you really cannot change them at the moment; worrying or criticising does not help.

Don't Take on Too much.

You need to have a balance and take your thoughts one step at a time. When you are up, you may try to take on too much. This is a way to recompensate for all previous failings. Divide your bigger goals into small daily goals and choose one big goal to focus on at a time. You need to eat an elephant piece by piece.

Don't Try to Be Perfect.

Realise that it is not all or nothing. Nothing is bad or good. Most of the time, we fail, and this is to teach us a lesson. Analyse the failings and learn that you need to step up or take a step back. Society teaches us that most successful people "came out of nowhere or they are lucky". But this is not the case. The most successful people worked hard for what they have, but this is rarely promoted. Realise that making mistakes is part of the journey and that you do not need to be perfect. Thomas Edison failed 2,774 times before he perfected the light bulb. So, do not be discouraged by setbacks.

How to improve well being:

Even though it feels like your pain will never end, suicidal thoughts often are caused by treatable health problems. These include physical and medical conditions such as depression. Depression is a serious condition; It affects the chemicals in your brain, which relate to mood and emotions.

Sufferers find it impossible or hard to feel happy, see solutions to their problems or even remember good times. If you have had treatment for depression in the past, it might be better to try other treatments to find one that works for you. Some practical things you can do when you are having suicidal thoughts include:

•Reach out and get help: Start by making a call to the Samaritans Helpline – You are not alone. You may feel like your loved one's do not care, but people want to help you.

•Tell someone what is going on. Call a friend or family member, doctor, or someone at your local church.

•Avoid all those things that might trigger your suicidal thoughts. Such triggers will be different for everyone. Some of the common triggers include things such as being alone, doing drugs or drinking alcohol.

•Promise yourself to find the time and courage to ask for help and seek treatment.

- Make your home safe; get rid of all temptations such as drugs, alcohol, or anything that you are planning to use or have used in the past to hurt yourself.

- Spending time with family or friends also will help as it will take your mind off suicidal thoughts. Time is on your side if you create it. So, allow yourself time! Do not act on any of the suicidal thoughts right away.

- Get plenty of sleep, and learn to deal with stress. Find and do things that you enjoy.

- If you are taking medication to treat depression, do not skip your medicine and take the right dose at the right time.

- Take care of your health and wellness. Follow your doctor's eating and exercise advice.

- Work with a professional. This could be a psychiatrist or a counsellor.

Be open with the professional who is looking after you! Tell them how you are feeling without holding back!

Chapter 8 - Self-Healing

It is the recovery process (generally from psychological disturbances or trauma), motivated by and directed by the patient, often guided only by instinct. This process encounters mixed fortunes due to its amateur nature, although self-motivation is a significant asset. Self-healing benefits lie in its ability to be tailored to the individual's unique experience and requirements. The process can be helped and accelerated by self-analysis techniques such as meditation.

The different meanings of self-healing:

It is the ultimate phase of Gestalt Therapy. Self-healing may refer to the body's automatic self-controlled repair processes. In a figurative sense, self-healing properties refer to systems or processes, which tend to correct any disturbances brought into them by nature or design. For example, the skin's regeneration after a cut or scrape or of an entire limb; In this case, the injured party (the living body) repairs the damaged part by themselves. Beyond the self-healing capacities of the physical body, many psychological factors can influence self-healing.

The Greek physician Hippocrates, who is known by many as the father of medical treatment, observed, "The physician must be ready, not only to accomplish his duty by himself but also to secure the cooperation of the patient, his attendants and externals." - Hippocrates.

Self-healing is a result of deliberately applied psychological mechanisms. These approaches may improve the mental and physical conditions of a person. Research shows that this results from numerous mechanisms, including relaxation, breathing exercises, fitness exercises, imagery, meditation, yoga, Qigong, tai chi, biofeedback, and some forms of psychotherapy, among other approaches.

What is self-healing?

Healing means becoming complete, more able to do what you wish to accomplish, and more able to enjoy your life. This wholeness may involve healing a physical wound, an emotional disturbance, a maladaptive behaviour (addiction, shyness, rage) or conflictual relationships. You **can** learn how to heal yourself. Healing is an active, living process.

Medicines, supplements, surgery and exercise, all help but are only support for the self-healing process. Antibiotics can weaken bacteria, but just your immune system can kill and get rid of them. Studies show that the most critical thing you can do is learn to create mental and physical relaxation and balance. Combined with guided imagery, meditation and self-hypnosis, these very potent mind tools will help you on your journey to a healthy physical and mental wellbeing.

Patient, Heal Thyself

The process of self-healing requires the adoption of actions that cause your internal system to function better and heal you faster. These include behaving wisely, tuning into the actual needs of your body, mind, spirit and soul, and making wise choices such as eating the right way, exercising, and getting the right amount of sleep. Practising the art of deep relaxation for ten or twenty minutes each day, three times a day, if you want, yields impressive and real results.

Focus on peace, beauty, harmony, love and other similar experiences.

Meditation and other deep relaxation techniques will help you to eliminate distractions. During this time, allow yourself to feel complete self-acceptance and the world just as it is at this moment- after all, it cannot be any different from how it is right now!

Flood your mind with the things you feel grateful for and have experienced.

Feel the gratitude in your body and be thankful; visualise your body, healing itself and becoming more functional. Then picture yourself as entirely thriving, healthy and happy. Do it several times a day to unlock the secrets of self-healing!

Self-healing Stress

Stress is an essential part of most of our illnesses. For some, it causes; for others, it makes it work. Some of the by-products of stress include:

•Mental stress produced disordered (incoherent) neural impulses in the nerves and circulates stress chemicals, in the body, that cause health problems such as inflammation.

•Muscle pain and dysfunction (backache, muscle tension, elevated blood pressure, chronic disorders)

•It leads to emotional imbalances such as irritability, anxiety, anger, unhappiness, and depression.

•It leads to mental dysfunction (low creativity, insomnia, procrastination, attention deficit)

•Stress contributes to behavioural disorders such as drinking, smoking or overeating.

•Chronic stress over a long period shrinks the brain, killing neurons by the millions.

A deeply relaxed state of mind re-balances the system. Most imbalances and disorders are either caused or made worse by physical tension and mental stress. Practising deep relaxation techniques is the direct antidote to stress and is thus widely used in self-healing. So, speed up your healing, and be sure to wisely guide the mind, thoughts, and emotions to function in a congruent way with the healing process you want to facilitate. In other words, be the change you want to create.

What is the Self-Healing Process?

Ancient Eastern medical models rely on energy because we have self-healing programmed in our bodies. We see this in action, for example, when we get a cut or scrape on our bodies. To change our lives physically, mentally, emotionally, and spiritually, we must tune into our energy body; it is a simple but effective process that can truly change our lives.

Is self-healing complicated?

You can take a few steps to bring a feeling of peace into your body. Tune into your body's energy; use your emotions and thoughts to change your energy frequency and flow. It is simple to change the channel from a negative reporting news channel to your favourite comedy show and feel relaxed with that change. The self-healing process can be very similar.

Can your body really self heal?

The human body naturally heals itself. From renewable cells to emotional healing, your body is capable of self-healing in many ways! We can learn to amplify our natural self-healing mechanisms by tuning into the process. We can learn to improve our innate self-healing abilities by learning to channel our bodies' energy. The energy healing experience is unique to any person who attempts to try it.

Most people who experience energy healing describe it as calming, comfortable, and physically friendly. However, if you are thinking of undergoing the energy-healing process, you should be ready for energy shifts and mood swings in your body.

What does energy healing feel like?

The healing energy experience is unique to each person who tries it. Many of those who have gone through it describe it as a relaxing, warm, and physically pleasant experience. Some incredible ways to self heal your body and mind Self-healing is not as complex as you think. Channelling your body's energy is fast and straightforward. Try channelling your body's energy and use your thoughts and feelings to alter your energy frequency. You should proceed in a unique direction to ensure you embrace, ease, breeze and even bring "magic" into your life.

A firm intention can change your life physically, mentally, emotionally, and spiritually. Here are five simple techniques to self-heal your body and mind:

Find a comfortable seat and concentrate on your breath:

No need to adjust your breathing pattern; pay close attention to the flow; inhale, and exhale. No decision, no change; Just observe! You will feel alive and avoid any mind-boggling thoughts from entering your mind for the next few moments.

Keep your hands (Palms together) in front of you and Rub them Rapidly for 30 – 60 seconds:

Warm your hands using friction. Smile as you rub your hands and make the most of this time about yourself. Remember smiling itself is soothing and can change your mood within seconds.

Feel the flow of energy by holding your hands 6-8 inches away:

This energy has always been there. All it needed was the same briefing of your intention and awakening of your consciousness. You feel this energy channelling inside you. Remember: that's part of you. Stay positive - doesn't it feel fantastic?

Close your eyes, try to transfer energy into your body:

Try to awaken your body's energy in your way; there is no such thing as doing it the wrong way. See if you can transfer the power through some part of your body. You may experience tension while doing so. Hold it there! You are giving your body healing energy and some well-deserved love. If you feel like you are losing contact with sensing the energy, rub your hands together once again.

No judgments are involved, and there is no wrong approach! Imagine the energy in a way that serves you the best. Maybe you want to experience it, or perhaps you want to imagine it as a white light; Experiment with this move and smile while doing it.

Continue working with this surge of energy:

Transfer the energy to various parts of your body. Observe how it feels entering different parts. This energy will strengthen those parts that generally bring pain; feel grateful for finally realising this innate ability. Feel the calming strength of the body's functions. Congratulate yourself for waking up to this consciousness and healing.

Working with this flow for only ten minutes will bring a sense of joy and peace you might have thought was impossible just minutes before. Now question yourself, how did it feel? When you first experienced this energy, are you amazed by the fact that this energy was present in your body all along, and you had done nothing about it? For just ten minutes, you can alter your energy flow and condition. It is in your power to heal your body, mind, and spirit.

Chapter 9 - Boost your self-esteem and create better habits

From time to time, most people feel bad about themselves. Feelings of low self-esteem are always triggered by being treated poorly by someone else recently or in the past or by a person's judgments of him or herself. However, such feelings are normal. Too many people who experience depression, anxiety, phobias, psychosis, delusional thinking, or those who have an illness, or a disability tend to have low self-esteem as a constant companion.

If you belong to this category, you may go through life feeling needlessly bad about yourself. Having low self-esteem keeps you from enjoying life, and working toward personal goals and stops you from doing the things you want to do, We all have a right to feel good about ourselves; however, it might be challenging to feel good about yourself if you are under stress.

The same can be said, for example, if you are dealing with a disability or if you have someone who is treating you badly. At these times, it is easy to dive deeper into a downward spiral of lower self-esteem. You may, for example, begin feeling bad about yourself when someone insults you, if you are having difficulty getting along with someone in your family, or are under much pressure at work. As a result, you then begin to give yourself negative self-talk like, "I am not good." This may get worse to the extent that you start doing things to hurt yourself or someone else. Some common pitfalls may include doing things such as getting drunk or yelling at your children.

By using the ideas and activities outlined below, you will equip yourself with advice on how to avoid doing things that make you feel even worse and do those things that will make you feel better about yourself. This chapter will give you ideas on things you can do to better yourself to raise your self-esteem.

These ideas have come from people like yourself, who realise they have low self-esteem and want to improve. You will start seeing improvements in your self-esteem as you begin to use the methods outlined in this book. It is normal to swing from feelings of resistance to positive feelings about yourself. Any negative feelings you might have will soon diminish as you start feeling better and better about yourself.

One thing that will relieve these feelings is to let your friends know what you are going through. Cry if you need to do so. Try and do things to relax, such as meditating or taking a nice warm bath. As you read through this chapter, remember this statement and keep telling yourself: "I am a very unique, special, and valuable individual. I deserve to be happy!"

Self-esteem, Depression and Other Illnesses

Low self-esteem may be due to depression; in fact, low self-esteem is a symptom of depression. Conversely, depression may be a symptom of some other underlying illness. If you have felt sad consistently for several weeks but do not know why you feel so bad, i.e., nothing bad has happened or you have not been able to shake off these feelings of sadness; you are likely suffering from depression. The other tell-tell signs could include:

- Wanting to eat all the time or having no appetite,

- Wanting to sleep all the time,

- Waking up very early, and

- Not getting back to sleep at all.

Immediate actions to improve self-esteem

Start Eating healthy and avoid junk foods containing a lot of sugar, salt or bad fats). A balanced daily diet is usually five or six servings of vegetables and fruit, and servings of whole-grain foods like bread, pasta, cereal, and rice. It is recommended that you eat around two servings of protein foods, chicken, fish, cheese, cottage cheese or yoghurt.

Exercise regularly

To feel better and improve your self-esteem, you need to move your body regularly. Arrange a time every day when you can get some exercise, probably outdoors. You can do many different things that constitute exercise. These range from taking a walk, going for a run, riding a bicycle, playing a sport, climbing up and down stairs several times, playing the radio and dancing to music, or anything else that makes you raise your heartbeat. If you have a health problem that may prevent you from exercising, check with your doctor for the most appropriate exercise alternatives for your condition.

Personal hygiene

Looking after your hygiene will make you feel better about yourself; this could include doing things such as having regular showers or baths, washing and styling your hair, trimming your nails, and brushing and flossing your teeth. Have a physical examination every year to ensure you are in good health and plan fun activities for yourself. Learn new things every day.

Take time to do things you enjoy

You may be so busy or feel bad about yourself and you spend little time or no time doing things you enjoy. You may find activities such as playing a musical instrument, doing a crafts project, fishing or even going for a run, very rewarding. A good starting point is to make a list of things you enjoy doing, then do something from that list, adding to the list anything new you discover along the way.

It is about time you got that something you have been putting off done!

Clean out that drawer, wash that window or write a letter or even pay that bill.

Use your special abilities and talents to do the things you enjoy

For example, if you are good with your hands, make something for yourself, friends or family.

If you are an animal lover, consider having a pet or playing with friends' pets.

Dress to your heart's desire!

Try dressing in clothes that make you feel good about yourself and if money is an issue, check out charity shops/thrift stores near your area for some bargains.

Reward yourself

You are a great person, and you deserve to treat yourself once in a while; before you go to bed, write about how well you treated yourself today.

Avoid negative people

Give your time to those who make you feel good about yourself—people who treat you well and avoid people who treat you badly.

Make your living space a place that owns the person you are

Whether you live in a single room, a small apartment or in a large home? Rearrange your space by making it look comfortable and attractive for you. In situations where you share your living space with others, have some space that is just for you, an undisturbed space where you can keep your things and one you can decorate according to your taste and liking. If you have the space, get some plants, and make sure they are safe for your pets too if you have them. Plants can liven up your personal space and offer a very calming environment for you to be in. It also gives you something else to focus on and distracts you.

Display items that you find attractive or remind you of your achievements or people or special times in your life. Using your creative skills could be an inexpensive or free way to add your personal touch to your space's comfort and enjoyment.

Spice up your mealtime!

Even when you are eating alone, turn off the television, radio or phone. Light a candle or place an attractive object in the centre of the table or even some flowers. Attractively arrange food on your plate and if you eat with others, encourage discussion of pleasant topics. Avoid discussing difficult issues at mealtimes.

Consider going to a seminar or signing up for a class

Many educational programmes are free of charge or are inexpensive. For those that are more costly, ask for a possible scholarship or fee reduction.

Do something charitable or a nice gesture

Say a few kind words to a random person; Smile at someone who looks sad. Help a spouse or family member with an unpleasant chore. Take a card to an acquaintance, Volunteer for a worthy cause. Make a meal for a friend who is sick. Random acts of kindness not only make us feel good about ourselves, but they can have a massive positive impact on other people's lives at the same time.

Chapter 10 - Turn Negative Thoughts into Positive Ones

Many people give themselves negative messages through self-talk. These messages may have started, or you learned them when you were young. They may have come from different sources, including other children while you were at school, your teachers, family members, caregivers, or social media. You may also have learned from prejudice and stigma in our society. You may have repeated these negative messages over and over to yourself, especially when you are not feeling well or while you are having a hard time.

Sometimes this is worsened by making up some negative messages of our own, messages which tend to lower one's self-esteem and make them feel bad about themselves. Examples of such negative messages that people repeat over and over to themselves include:

"I am an idiot",

"I never do anything right",

"No one would ever like me",

"I am a loser."

The hard part is, that self-talk usually feels genuine, and we tend to believe it even when it is biased, untrue or unreal. Negative thoughts tend to come up immediately in the right circumstances; for example, if you get a wrong answer to a question, you think, "I am so stupid", You might be saying things like, "I should have known the answer to that question." These thought processes tend to make you imagine the worst in everything; they are often hard to turn off or unlearn. Some people are giving themselves these messages so often that they are hardly aware of them.

Practical Steps to counter negative thoughts:

✓ Firstly, start by paying attention to these negative thoughts. Carry out a little self-audit. Get a small pad that you can carry along as you go about your daily routine, or create a note on your smartphone, for several days, jot down negative thoughts about yourself each time you notice them. You might notice negative thinking when you are tired, dealing with stress or when you are sick. Because they are written down, you will start noticing patterns as well as the frequency with which they occur.

✓ To check if they are true, take a closer look at your audit; you might even get a counsellor or a close trusted friend to help you with this.

✓ Reflect on some of the negative thoughts by asking yourself some of the following questions about each negative thought you have noticed; it might help if you do this when you are in a good mood or are feeling positive: Is it true? What did I get out of thinking this way? If this way of thinking makes me feel bad about myself, why not stop? Is there any evidence for and against my thinking?

How can I find out if what I am thinking is true? Can I look at this situation in a different light? Will I achieve my goals if I continue thinking this way? Can I learn anything from this situation to help me do better next time?

✓ Often, reflecting or just looking at a thought or situation in a new light or with a fresh pair of eyes, is what it takes to rectify our negative thought process.

✓ Start developing positive statements you can say to yourself to counter these negative thoughts. Start using phrases that include positive words like happy, loving, enthusiastic, warm and peaceful.

✓ Stay clear of negative words such as worried, frightened, upset, tired, bored, never, can't. Do not make a statement like "I am not going to worry anymore." Try saying, "I am focusing on the positive". Always use present tense, e.g. "I am happy, I have a good job, I am healthy, I am well" as if the condition already exists. Use your name, I, or me.

✓ Make your ideas visible by putting them on a piece of paper. Fold a piece of paper in half on the long edge and make two columns. Write your negative thought in one column and write a positive belief that contradicts the negative ones in the other column. You can change your negative thoughts to positive ones by replacing them with positive ones every time you realise you are thinking about a negative idea. Repeating aloud whenever you get a chance or sharing your positive thoughts can lead to significant benefits.

Summary of practical tips to help you stay positive:

• Write down your thoughts and challenge negative ones with positive ones.

• Make signs that say a positive thought.

• Hang your pieces of paper with positive thoughts in places where you would see them often, like your refrigerator door or on a bathroom mirror and repeat them several times to yourself when you see them.

• To reinforce the positive thought, repeat it over and over to yourself when you are deeply relaxed, for example, when you are doing relaxation exercises such as meditation, falling asleep, deep breathing exercises or when you are waking up.

• Learning to challenge the negative thoughts about yourself with positive ones takes time and persistence, but it is worth the effort. If you use the techniques above consistently for four to six weeks, you will notice that you do not think these negative thoughts about yourself as much as you did. If they recur at some time, you can repeat these activities. You deserve to think and feel good about yourself. Do not give up!

Chapter 11 - Feel Good activities

The following activities will, in the long run, improve your self-esteem. Do what seems most comfortable to you. You may want to alternate between activities, and for some, you may get better benefits if you repeat them regularly.

Make Affirming lists

Making lists, regularly reading them, and re-writing them from time to time, will help you feel better about yourself. If you have a diary or journal or even a note-taking application on your phone, you can make your lists on that, or if you prefer a traditional piece of paper, that will do.

Make a list of:

• Focus on your top five positive strengths, e.g., Courage, persistence, creativity, friendliness, or resilience.

• Five things you admire about yourself – these could include your morals, the way you raise or raised your children, and the good relationship you have with a loved one.

• Some of your greatest achievements in your life so far. These could include graduating from high school, recovering from an illness, or learning a new skill.

• At least 20 accomplishments – could be as simple as learning to tie your shoelaces to something like completing a college degree.

• 10 Ways you can reward or treat yourself – include simple, inexpensive things such as a walk in the woods, window shopping, and chatting with a friend.

• 10 things that can make you laugh.

• 10 things you can do to help someone in need.

Exercise to Reinforce a positive self-image.

✓ To do this task, you need a piece of paper, a pen or pencil and a clock or timer. Any paper will do, but it is even better if you have your favourite pen and paper.

✓ Set your alarm for 10 minutes.

✓ Across the top of the page, add your name.

✓ Now write something positive and good. Include characteristics and talents, and achievements.

✓ You can use single words or phrases, whichever you prefer. It is ok to repeat some of the things to emphasize them. Do not worry about spelling or grammar. Your ideas also do not have to be organized. Keep writing down whatever comes to your mind; remember you are the only person who will see this paper. Avoid any negative statements or the use of negative words and phrases.

✓ When the time is up, read the paper over to yourself. You might feel sad when you read it over because it is a new, and different but positive way of thinking about yourself. It may contradict some of the negative thoughts that you may have had about yourself.

✓ As you read this paper, those negative feelings will diminish. Go over it several times and put it somewhere convenient such as your pocket, purse, wallet or table or even on your bedside table.

✓ Please read it to yourself several times a day to keep reminding yourself how great you are. You may also read it to a good friend or family member who is supportive; you may also find a comfortable place and read it out to yourself aloud.

Developing positive affirmations

Affirmations are positive statements that you can make about yourself, to feel better. They are descriptions of the way you would like to feel about yourself at the time. However, they may not describe how you might be feeling about yourself right now. Consider the following affirmations that will help you when making your own list:

• I find it easy to get along with my colleagues.

- I am naturally motivated and driven.
- I feel good about myself.
- I am healthy.
- I do things I enjoy.
- I keep my thoughts positive and healthy.
- My body is strong, fit and healthy.

More Positive Affirmations

- I spend time with people who are nice to me and make me feel good about myself.
- I choose to eat foods that are good for me.
- I am a good person.
- I deserve to be alive.
- Many people like me
- I take care of my body and exercise daily.
- I am dedicated to improving my vitality and health.
- I am living here in vitality.
- My immune system is strong.
- I always make healthy choices.

Please make a list of your own affirmations and keep it in a handy place such as your purse or pocket. Duplicate the list and keep copies in separate places just in case you lose the original. Read your affirmations over and over to yourself aloud whenever you can. You may also share them with others whenever you feel comfortable doing so. Over time you will notice that your affirmations will tend to become true gradually, and consequently, you will feel better about yourself.

Develop a "Celebration's scrapbook."

Put together a scrapbook that celebrates you and the wonderful person you are. Have fun making it by including a picture of yourself, writings or quotes you enjoy, mementoes of things you have done or places you have been, pictures of yourself at different ages, awards, or cards you have received. Set up a special place in your home that celebrates you. Do not overcomplicate it; a table or shelf you can decorate with objects that remind you of the special person you are will do. If you cannot find a private space, then put the objects in a special box and set them up whenever you wish. Whenever you feel like bolstering your self-esteem, take them out and look at them.

Self-Esteem Calendar

Find a calendar or chart with large blank spaces for each day. On each day, schedule something small you would enjoy doing, such as calling your sister, sketching a cat, going into the flower shop and smelling the flowers, telling a loved one how much you love them, baking brownies, wearing your favourite scent, lie in the sun for 20 minutes. Commit to a "self-esteem calendar" every day and do whatever you have scheduled.

Mutual complementing exercise

If you have a friend or relative that is in a similar situation as yourself, then you can try an exercise that will make you both feel better about yourselves.

• Get together for 10 minutes with a friend or person you like and trust.

• Set a timer for five minutes or note the time on your watch. One of you begins complimenting the other person. It would be best if you were saying positive things to each other in turns.

• Notice how you feel about yourself before and after this exercise. Repeat it as often as you wish.

Chapter 12 - Break the chain with mindfulness meditation

Worry and Pre-Worrying:

People with stress and anxiety often become subject to negative thinking, constant worry, and anxious feelings. For example, most people with a panic disorder have time to worry and fear about the future. Some people pre-worry about things or situations that are in the future, trying to prepare themselves for the worst, when the situation hasn't arisen yet, but pre-worry about it, just in case they need to worry about it later. They feel that because they have pre-worried about the situation, they are better prepared for the worst outcome and will be able to deal with it easier, as they have already worried about it and are expecting it. In reality, the actual situation rarely happens, and they spent a lot of time upset, anxious and worried for no reason.

Luckily, methods for calming can help to offset these signals. Relaxation techniques are strategies that can be learned by yourself or with a professional guide. Such exercises are designed to help you calm down your thoughts, relieve pressure and open up for deep relaxation.

These strategies can help counter many of the panic disorder and anxiety's cognitive and physical effects. Deep breathing, visualization, massage, yoga, and progressive muscle relaxation (PMR) are the prevalent relaxation techniques. Mindfulness meditation is another prevalent relaxation ability that can help to reduce stress and anxiety.

What Is Mindfulness Meditation?

Meditation is a technique of relaxation that restores your consciousness to the present. The meditator encourages ideas to emerge during the practice of meditation without trying to stop or evaluate them. Unpleasant ideas, for example, concerning fear, conviction, guilt, and concern, may arise. Mindfulness is the practice of understanding and allowing such thoughts to go by. The idea that most people are driving away or ignoring their present thoughts and sentiments is based on mindfulness meditation. Most claim that these feelings simply disappear if they suppress negative thoughts. However, focus allows you to separate yourself from negative thinking without reaction.

Getting Started:

It can be useful to do in an area free of distractions when you first begin to practice consciousness meditation. Your individual needs may be dictated by the time of day you choose to meditate. Some people prefer meditation to start their day, reduce anxiety in the morning and set a clear and positive tone for the day, for example. Some would rather meditate at night, stop the pressure of the day, and brace themselves for the rest of the night.

Many forms of meditation also involve concentration–repeating a phrase and concentrating on the sensation of breathing which enables the procession of thoughts to come and go. The well-known calming mechanism can be triggered by focus meditation techniques, as well as other exercises such as Tai Chi and yoga, which are very useful when minimising the stress response. Mindfulness meditation draws on practices of concentration and can be extremely fulfilling.

This is how it functions:

Go with the flow.

As you focus, you follow the movement of inner thoughts, feelings, and corporeal experiences, without finding them good or bad in consciousness meditation. You should be alone when you first start to practice meditation, or with a trusted person with whom you feel completely relaxed and not self-conscious around.

Pay attention.

You can also note external feelings like noises, sights, and touches that make up your experience every moment. The goal is not to get stuck in worrying about the past, or the future, with particular ideas, sentiments, and feelings. You instead look around and discover the psychological habits that produce a sense of well-being or suffering.

Stay with it.

In some cases, this cycle may not seem calming at all, but over time, it provides you with a broader range of experiences and provides a path to more happiness and self-consciousness. Mindfulness meditation may seem trivial enough, but it is hard from time to time for even daily meditators. When they first sit down to meditate, many people experience heightened anxiousness. Motivation and desire can also diminish every day, so seek to be gentle with yourself and relax. You'll learn to sit with uncomfortable thoughts if you keep to your meditation practice. Only by regular practice can awareness meditation become less difficult, help you decrease anxiety and make you feel relaxed.

Breathing Exercises

You can try to alleviate symptoms and start feeling better when you feel breathless from stress or anxiety. These are some of the things you can try to incorporate into your daily life, to help you to change your focus and calm your mind.

1. Lengthen Your Exhale

You can relax yourself simply by inhaling. A deep breath is linked to the sympathetic nervous system that controls the reaction to fight and flight. Yet exhalation is related to the nervous parasympathetic system which inhibits the capacity of our body to calm and heal.

Try a thorough exhale before you take a big, deep breath. Drive the oxygen out of your body and then just let your lungs inhale air for their job. First, try to exhale a little more than you breathe. Exhale for six, for example, inhale for 4 seconds. About two to five minutes to do that, no more. You can do this any way you are comfortable, like standing, sitting or lying, whichever is convenient for you.

2. Abdomen Breathing

Breathing from the diaphragm (the muscle that is under your lung) can help reduce the amount of work your body needs to do. These are some methods of diaphragm breathing:

• Lie down on a floor or mattress under your head and knees with pillows for warmth. Or sit down and relax your head, neck and shoulders in a comfortable chair and bend your knees.

• You put your hand under your rib cage and your heart with one hand.

• Inhale and exhale your nose, realizing how or whether you breathe and move your stomach and chest.

• You should separate the breath so that the air gets absorbed into your lungs, pause, and then breathe out. Could you feel your chest moving when you breathe? So rather than your chest, you want your stomach to move while you breathe.

Practice belly breathing

• As described above, sit or lie down.

• Place one hand behind your neck and the other on the abdomen (your tummy).

• Breathe in via your nose and feel your belly rise Your chest will stay fairly still.

• Purse your lips and breathe out via the mouth. Try to push the air out at the end of the breath using your stomach muscles. You must practice it daily to make this type of breathing automatic. Try to practice for up to 10 minutes three or four times a day. You may feel tired at first if you haven't used your diaphragm to breathe. However, with practice, it will become easier.

3. Breath Focus in practice

It can help reduce anxiety if deep breathing is focused and slow. By sitting or lying in a quiet, comfortable location, you can do this technique. Try the following:

- Notice the sensation when you normally inhale and exhale. Take time to concentrate on the breathing motion. You will feel the tension you've never felt in your body.

- Through your nose, take a deep and slow breath.

- Notice the expansion of your lower abdomen and upper body.

- Exhale in any manner that's right for you, sighing if you want.

- Take care of the rise and fall of your stomach for a few minutes.

- Pick a word during your exhalation to concentrate and vocalize. Terms such as 'security' and 'calm' can work.

- Imagine looking at the air you inhale like a soft wave over you.

- Imagine your exhalation, which takes away negative, upsetting thoughts and energy.

- Bring your attention to your breath and your words softly when you get upset. Use this method, if possible, for up to 20 minutes every day.

4. Equal Breathing

Another form of respiration deriving from ancient pranayama yoga practice is equal breath. This means that you drink the same way you breathe. A clear space and lying down help you to practice equal breathing. Regardless of your position, be sure you are comfortable.

• Close your eyes and be careful how many breaths you normally breathe.

• Then count 1-2-3-4 slowly, as you breathe in with your nose.

• Breathe out for the same count of four seconds.

• Be mindful of the sensations of fullness and absence in your body when you inhale and exhale. When you continue to practice equal breathing, the second count can be whatever you're comfortable with, but keep the inhalation and exhalation counts both the same.

5. Resonant Breathing

Resonant breathing will help you relieve your fear and get you into a relaxed position, often called coherent breathing. Please try it yourself:

• Lie down and shut your eyes.

• Breathe in via your nose gently leaving the mouth closed and count for six seconds.

• Don't overfill the air with your lungs.

• Breathe out for six seconds, so that the air slowly and gently leaves your body. Don't push it.

- Keep going for up to 10 minutes.

- Make sure you are still for a few more minutes and focus on the feeling of your body.

6. Lion's Breath

The breath of the Lion means powerful exhalation. To practice the breath of a lion:

- Get into a spot to kneel, cross your knees, and rest your legs. Sit cross-legged, if this position is not comfy.

- Pull your palms out, and extend your legs and feet to your thighs.

- Take a gentle breath in through your mouth.

- Open your mouth as wide as you can during exhale and stick out your tongue as far as possible.

- Breathe out fast through your nose.

- Concentrate on the centre of your forehead (third eye) or the end of your nose while you breathe.

- Gently inhale again, through your mouth.

- Repeat up to six times, switch your legs over to cross them the other way when you arrive at the halfway stage.

7. Alternate Nostril Breathing

Sit in a comfortable place to try repeating our nose breathing, sit up straight to stretch your spinal cord and open your chest. Place your left hand comfortably in your lap and raise your right hand in front of your face. Then place your index finger and middle fingers together on your forehead between the eyebrows.

• Close your eyes, and deeply inhale and exhale through your nose.

• Use your right thumb to shut your right nostril and slowly inhale with the left nostril.

• Pinch your nose between your right index finger and thumb and hold your breath for a second.

• Lift your right thumb and exhale through your right nostril and wait a moment before inhaling again.

• Inhale through your right nostril slowly.

• Close both your nostrils again for a second, stop.

• Then, open and exhale on your left nostril and wait until you're ready to inhale again.

• Repeat this inhalation and exhalation process up to 10 times through either nostril.

Consistency is key here, so try to breathe in and out at equal lengths.

You should feel balanced and calm.

8. Guided Meditation

Guided meditation is used to relieve anxiety by breaking thinking patterns that maintain tension. Sitting or lying in a warm, quiet, relaxing and peaceful position could lead you into a guided meditation. Then listen to soothing recordings and relax your body and breathe. Guided meditation recordings, apps and videos allow you to see a calmer and less stressful reality. It can also help you to control intrusive thinking that causes anxiety.

There is a world of guided meditation videos and apps available on almost every platform. Many are free, like YouTube videos or free apps, and some are not. I would highly recommend using the free trials and free videos to experiment with the different styles of guided meditation, to see which works for you best. Everyone is different and will connect to different methods. When you have found a method that suits you best, then it may be worth considering a purchase if you cannot find enough content in your favourite style, but there should be plenty of free ones available, and you can always use the same one over and over if it works well for you.

Use one or more of these above breathing techniques to see if it can relieve your symptoms when you have depression or panic attacks. If your symptoms persist or increase, then arrange a date with your doctor or psychiatrist. You should never ignore your symptoms. With the help and the right solutions for you, you will restore your quality of life and control your symptoms.

Mindfulness Tricks to Reduce Anxiety:

Anxiety will fatigue you emotionally and affect your body effectively. Before you worry about anxiety, however, know that the research shows that with simple attention training you can reduce your anxiety and stress. Pay attention to daily life and the things that you normally run through. It's a matter of changing the mind's amplitude by returning calmness to the brain.

Don't think too hard, you don't have to spend an hour paying for a yoga course or distort your body in tough positions. You have probably all the equipment you require to practice mindfulness. Use these tricks to create small explosions of consciousness during the day to relieve fear and relax the mind.

Set An Intention

Try to make your practice, an intention on that day. Whether you do it before your breakfast or before important events, you can focus and remember why you are doing something by setting an intention. Set an intention for something that gives you anxiety— like a big talk at work. For example, before going to a sports centre or treating your body with kindness, you can set an intention of looking after your body.

Do A Guided Meditation Or Mindfulness Practice

Meditation can be as straightforward as opening an app. Online programs and apps are a great way to get your teeth into an activity without spending a lot of time on a costly course. Innumerable private, guided meditations are available online. These apps for meditation are an excellent starting point, and many can be found by simply searching on YouTube.

Doodle Or Color

Relax your brain with a doodle for a few minutes. You can let your creative juices flow and give your brain a break. Invest in a colouring book, whether adult or not. They are a great way to change your focus and wake up the creative side of your brain, without having to be artistic.

Go For A Walk

Being outside is wonderful for anxiety. Be vigilant about the sounds, the sensation of the breeze on your body, and the smells. Keep your mobile in your pocket and do your best for your senses and the environment to remain in the moment. Start around the block with a short jaunt, see how you're feeling.

Wish Other People Happiness

This training by Chade-Meng Tan, a former investor of Google, takes you just 10 seconds to complete. All through the day, spontaneously wish for someone to be delighted. You do not have to tell it to the person, you can keep the thoughts to yourself, the positive energy is all you have to bring. Try it while on your bus, in the workplace, in the gym or even while waiting in line. Bonus points if you're angry and frustrated with somebody and you pause and wish them good luck.

Look Up

Not only from the monitor (although you definitely do) but also from the stars. When you take the trash out or come to your home late, stop by looking at the stars and take a few deep breaths into your stomach. Let the cosmos remind you that life is bigger than your problems or your inbox.

Brew On It

Making a cup of tea in many cultures around the world is a highly appreciated custom. Just settle in and concentrate on every step. If you take the leaves out, how can they smell? When you first add the coffee, what does the liquid feel like? See the steam coming out from the cup and touch your palm with the heat of the cup. Drink your tea with no distraction if you have time. Don't like tea? You can make rich, aromatic French pressed coffee easily with this method or a wholesome smoothie.

Focus On One Thing At A Time

Sure, if you do that right, your to-do list can be a form of attention. Set a minute timer and pay full and unequivocal attention to one task. No phone searching, no updates pressing, no web surfing-no multitasking whatsoever. Let one task be the focus of attention until the time is running out.

Leave Your Phone Behind

Do you actually need to take your mobile phone to the other room? When are you going to the toilet? When you are sitting to eat? Consider leaving your handset in the other room. Sit down and breathe before you start eating rather than worry about it. When you're finished, your phone will still be there.

Turn Household Tasks Into A Mental Break

Allow yourself to live in the moment rather than obsessing about your to-do list and debris. Dance when you make the dishes and focus on how the soap goes down during the washing of the tub. Take five slow breaths while waiting for a "ding" from the microwave. Daydream as you fold the laundry.

Journal

There is no right or wrong way to do this. The practice of putting thoughts on paper can help calm the mind and emotions, so scribble your ideas on a blank piece of paper. Write things that you are thankful for today or just jot down three of today's best events.

Pause At Stoplights

We all hate getting stuck in traffic. Instead of feeling anxious, when there is nothing you can do about traffic jams or every stoplight being red, sit upright and stand still while waiting and take 4 long, slow breaths. This technique sounds easy on a calm ride, but when the anxiety and stress feel like taking the whole car the real benefits will come.

Log Out Of All Of Your Social Media Accounts

Although social media has its advantages, it can also make your depression more powerful and hinder your performance. You will be surprised how often you check without thinking, your social networks accounts. Therefore, log out. You will slow down or stop outrightly when required to type a password again.

Set a time limit or intention when you want to check-in. In this way, you will not end up being behind on your job or guilty to look at a puppy for 20 minutes. Also, during the time you are there, you may want to delete an account or two. A recent study found that anxiety in young adults was linked to the use of multiple social media platforms.

Check Out

Poor focus will increase anxiety and stress. Know when you have to let go of some energy and allow your mind to wander. In your mindfulness practice, A good film and relaxation have their place but that won't work on its own. Every bit of mindfulness has its own benefits. The important thing is that you are in harmony with your philosophy of consciousness. According to a recent review, daily concentration training will help you relax your mind and transfer negative emotions. Seek to do a workout or a mindfulness exercise that is practised every day, for at least five minutes, and try to change it up, so you can try new methods and techniques.

Chapter 13 - Self-Confidence and Self-Belief

To indeed be self-confident is to radiate confidence in your words and actions in addition to believing in yourself and feeling capable.

The psychology of Self-Belief and Self-Confidence:

We have also learned that self-confidence is an essential predictor of success. William James' formula for self-esteem proposes two foundations:

- What we believe and feel about ourselves(Our self-confidence, self-belief)

- How we perform(Our successes)

James first laid out the detail for this concept; however, it is not limited to him; this idea influenced the work of a vital self-confidence and self-esteem theory known as the "Bandura's Self Efficacy Theory." This theory states that self-efficacy is built on your beliefs in the likelihood of future success. If you believe you can influence future events in your life, then you have high self-efficacy, whereas if you feel that you are not in control and have little to no impact on what happens to you in the future, then you have low self-efficacy (Bandura 1977).

Bandura's theory of self-efficacy is focused on current beliefs about the future. Self-confidence revolves around assumptions about the future, leading to the existence of a definite link to the past; after all, our self-confidence is built on our past experiences. Deci and Ryan drew from Bandura's work to create their theory on another self-construct that we now know as self-esteem. Self-determination theory states that self-esteem is a result of humanity's needs being met, and we are all born with an innate drive to explore our environments, and as a result, we thrive. This theory expands the boundaries of self-confidence by adding in the "needs" component.

According to this theory, if our needs are met, we have all the ingredients necessary to experience healthy self-esteem allowing us to grow and flourish. Based on these theories, and numerous articles, reports, and studies by other researchers in this field, we now have a more coherent picture of self-confidence. It is the feeling of self-assurance and a sense of self-belief in your ability to gain chances of future success.

Self-Esteem Vs Self-Confidence

Despite self-confidence and self-esteem crossing paths at many points and sharing some standard features, they are considered two distinct constructs. Self-esteem is a stable trait that does not change much in individuals. Unless they put in some dedicated effort to improve. It can generally be defined as a belief in our inherent worth, value and how deserving we are of happiness, success, love, and other exemplary aspects that add meaning to our lives. Self-confidence, by contrast, does not take into consideration any beliefs about the overall value or worthiness. It instead focuses on the ability to succeed and the thoughts about your ability to succeed. Clearly, the two are related, but it is easy to see where the distinction might lie. Self-confidence is about the success you feel that you can achieve, while self-esteem is about the success you deserve.

Using Therapy for treating cases of Lack of Self-Confidence

Among other forms of therapy, Cognitive Behaviour Therapy (CBT) is increasingly helpful in the treatment of low-self-confidence cases. It aims at changing dysfunctional thinking behavioural patterns and replacing them with healthy functional thinking patterns. The primary and most typical techniques used in CBT include:

- Graduted exposure

- Cognitive restructuring

- Mindfulness training

- Problem Solving

The Importance of believing in yourself:

Self-belief and self-confidence bring about many desirable benefits ranging from feeling good about yourself to many others, such as:

• Self-confident individuals can deal with stress and difficult times better, which leads to overall good health.

• People with good self-belief tend to spend more time with their friends and family since they set healthy boundaries and can adopt a healthy work-life balance.

• Better relationships thanks to healthy boundaries, resulting in the ability to focus on improving relationships and good communication.

• Improve performance at work as a result of an ability to concentrate, this leads to an improved commitment to tasks.

In addition to the above mentioned, below is a list of benefits that come from boosting your confidence. Some likely outcomes of greater self-confidence in yourself include:

• Improved coping and thriving under stress.

• Better ability to influence and persuade others.

• More leadership and executive presence.

• Increased positive attitude.

• Enhanced sense of feeling valued by others.

- Improve performance at work.

- Being perceived as more attractive.

- Reduced negative thoughts.

- More fearlessness and less anxiety.

- Greater freedom from social fear.

- Greater levels of happiness

- Increased energy and motivation.

Self-Limiting beliefs and Low Self-Confidence

On the flip side, when you have low confidence, the opposite of the above benefits tends to happen; struggles range from problems with work to issues with your relationships. Low self-confidence leads to feelings of unhappiness and inadequate mechanisms for coping with stress. This downward trend leads to a lack of energy and poor motivation. People with low self-confidence may also suffer from self-limiting beliefs; such constraints and beliefs may hinder you from doing the things that can help you grow and prosper. Self-limiting beliefs can fall into the following categories:

- I don't / I do -limiting beliefs regarding how we define ourselves.

- I can't -limiting beliefs in terms of our self-image and self-efficacy.

- I shouldn't / I should –limiting beliefs that keep us stuck in self-judgment and even self-shame

- I am not / I am -limiting beliefs that centre on what we are not or what we are, for example, "I am intelligent" vs "I am stupid."

- Others will/ Others are -limiting beliefs that focus on other people.

The Role of Self-Confidence in Relationships:

Believing in yourself plays a huge role in relationship satisfaction, both your own and that of your partner. A study on the effect of self-esteem on relationships and satisfaction found that an individual's self-esteem is a significant predictor of their relationship satisfaction; it is also a predictor of their partner's relationship satisfaction.

Those with a healthy level of self-esteem tended to have a secure attachment style and enjoyed greater satisfaction in their relationships, especially when they were in a relationship with another high self-esteem individual. The effect of self-belief on relationships is so significant it can even indicate alternative ways of thinking about your partner.

Studies on this topic found that those with low self-esteem are less able to integrate positive and negative thinking about their partner. They tend to fall prey to "all or nothing", and "black and white" thinking; either their relationship is fantastic, and their partner is terrific, or their partner is problematic, and their relationship is awful.

Healthy Self-Belief

Healthy self-belief is a realistic but optimistic evaluation of yourself and your abilities, a sense of trust and confidence in yourself. It is not about boasting or bragging. Here are some examples that illustrate healthy self-belief: Consider a scenario of a woman who has been on her first date and has had a great time; she believes they got on really well, and she is looking forward to their subsequent encounter. However, when he does not call within a few days, she refrains from falling into a negative thought spiral and instead thinks. "Maybe he is not the type of guy who calls right away. Or, maybe we just are not right for each other; all that matters is that I had fun."

In this alternative scenario, a man looking for a job sees an advert that has several requirements, he meets some, but he doesn't quite reach the cut off on a couple of them. Instead of passing it up due to the fear of never being shortlisted for the interview, he applies anyway, and during the interview, he explains how he has other traits that would make up for the qualifications he lacks, and he gets the job.

Finally, a student is interested in taking an Advanced Placement class at her college. She talks to her friends about it. Those who have already taken the same class tell her it is hard and that she probably would not pass. However, instead of using their judgments, she holds firm in her belief about her abilities, signs up anyway and with some hard work, aces the course.

General qualities of Self-confident individuals

Spotting self-confident people is not such a big challenge. There are plenty of signs that indicate that a person is confident and self-assured. Such signs include:

- They are willing to take risks and go the extra mile to get what they want.

- They can admit their mistakes and quite often can learn from those mistakes.

- They do not brag or boast about their accomplishments but wait for others to congratulate them

- They accept compliments with grace and gratitude.

In addition to these general signs, some signs are specific to relationships. Partners with self-confidence are:

- Less likely to be jealous and controlling.

- Willing to be vulnerable.

- Comfortable and ready to set healthy boundaries.

- Willing to admit when they are wrong.

- Comfortable assuming their date is like them.

- They are assured of their ability to make good decisions.

- They are likely to accept responsibility for their actions and emotions.

- They are willing to leave bad or unhealthy relationships.

Road map for building self-confidence skills:

To become like those people described above is not necessarily an easy road to walk. However, it is a worthy effort. If you feel you lack self-confidence, then here are some tips for building and boosting self-confidence and self-belief:

Prepare for a Journey.

- Take inventory of what you have already achieved.

- Think about your strengths and weaknesses.

- Think about your goals and values.

- Stop negative self-talk in its tracks by replacing it with positive thoughts.

- Give the journey to self-confidence your total commitment.

Setting out

- Enhance and identify the knowledge and skills you need to succeed.

- Focus on the basics – do not get bogged down in the details or trying to reach for perfection.

- Pile up successes by setting goals and achieving them. Even small wins, are wins and will boost your self-confidence.

- Continue working on positive self-talk and positive thoughts.

Head towards success

- Enjoy the fruits of your labour by celebrating your accomplishments.

- Keep yourself grounded.

- Take stock and assess your current level of self-confidence and identify areas for further improvement.

- If you hit roadblocks on your journey to self-confidence, don't worry! They happen to everyone. Try and work on ways how to get yourself back on track.

Steps for Boosting your self-confidence:

People who are confident about themselves tend to see themselves positively, and the way they feel dramatically influences how they live and interact with others. They do not feel awkward or self-conscious around others and tend to live happy and fulfilled lives. However, if you are drowning in the sea of hesitancy, self-doubt and shyness, you will avoid interacting, or connecting with people will be difficult, and in the end, you will withdraw and isolate yourself.

This type of anxiety you feel in the centre of your stomach when you are around people is holding you back considerably. It is not good for your emotional health and overall well-being. Confidence is walking into a room and not having to compare yourself to anyone; it is not about walking into a room and thinking you are better than everyone.

Here are some practical tips to boost your self-confidence right now and make yourself feel and act your best.

Stop labelling yourself with names like shy, awkward or timid!

Labelling yourself as shy, timid or awkward is compared to subconsciously telling your mind to psychologically feel inclined to live up to those expectations and act accordingly. Instead of labelling and entertaining negative self-talk, visualise and affirm yourself as confident and strong. Visualise yourself in a different situation you would like to be in - close your eyes for a minute if that helps. Experts believe that positive affirmations and good mental practices can lead to greater feelings of self-assurance, and they prepare the brain for success. Be your own cheerleader! Picture yourself winning or achieving your goals. Picture yourself as confident, and you will soon begin to manifest behaviour that gives evidence to this new fact. As the saying goes: "seeing is believing".

Recognise that the world is not focused on you!

That means you do not have to be excessively sensitive about who you are or what you are doing or not doing. As the rapper, Rocko, sings, "You just do you, and I will do me, right?" You are not at the centre stage! And there is no need for preoccupation with yourself and perfectionism. Trying to be perfect and a people pleaser puts too much pressure on you and creates unnecessary anxiety. Stop trying to please everyone or being perfect. Realise that other people are too preoccupied with their own issues, and they are not paying much attention to your every move except if you are a mega-famous, super celebrity.

Put the spotlight on other people as opposed to yourself.

If you are low on self-confidence, nervous, shy and self-conscious in social situations, then focus your attention on others. Listen to what they are saying or doing instead of focusing on your awkwardness. Think about what is interesting about the person who is at the centre of the party or that girl you are talking to all evening. Ask questions that will prompt them to tell you more about themselves; however, be genuinely curious and show interest in what they say. People generally want to talk about themselves or be heard and understood. You will instantly come across as warm-hearted and confident.

They will love it when you are eager and willing to listen to them or show interest in what they are saying. If you focus more on what you love in others as opposed to what you dislike in yourself; you will become more assertive and comfortable in social situations, but more importantly, it will make you feel great about yourself.

Know yourself for who you are

The Chinese philosopher and general, Sun Tzu, author of the "The Art of War", said: "Know yourself, and you will win all battles." To win your battle of lack of self-confidence, you will need to know yourself. This knowledge of yourself starts with understanding that all people are not the same. It also helps to understand that not all social situations are suitable for everyone. Someone who is not confident in large gatherings might be bold in one-to-one and small group interactions.

Everyone has their unique ways of expressing themselves, and that goes with their own unique gifts, embrace yours. Introverts have a quiet confidence that is unfortunately often confused for shyness. They prefer to spend time alone and are naturally low-key. On the flip side, this natural disposition affords them unique gifts, they can notice things that most others would not, and they listen better than others. Your strength and advantage lie in your uniqueness. You will not all the time be confident and comfortable in all social situations. "There is a genius in everybody!" - Albert Einstein

It helps to crack a smile

Cracking a smile is one of the fastest ways of boosting your confidence. Flashing those pretty, pearly white teeth will instantly make you appear both composed and confident. But the effects of smiling are not just external. It has been proven that smiling can also help negate the feeling of stress and give way to a happier and more relaxed you. That is not a bad return on such a simple and seemingly so subtle investment.

Break a sweat with Exercise.

Another great way to make yourself look good, feel amazing and improve your self-confidence is working out. Exercising increases your endorphins, which helps to reduce stress, tones your muscles, and makes you feel happy and confident. Can you imagine taking a few steps in the park will result in that feel-good feeling? It is all about whether you break a sweat or not to stimulate that endorphin production; it is not about how strenuous your session is; for many, that is a fantastic prospect.

Groom yourself.

This might seem like a mundane task, but it is incredible how much of a difference a shave and a shower can have on your self-confidence and self-image. As it turns out, your favourite fragrance does more than make you smell so nice. A scent can inspire confidence in men. Interestingly, studies have shown the more a man likes the fragrance, the more confident they might feel. 90% of women feel more confident when wearing a scent than those who go fragrance-free.

Dress Nicely

Another one that might seem corny but works; If you dress nicely, you will instantly feel good about yourself and give your self-confidence a real boost. That is because you will feel attractive, presentable, and sometimes even successful in nice clothes. While dressing nicely means something different, for example, it does not necessarily mean wearing expensive designer outfits. It means wearing clothes that are clean, comfortable, and make you feel good and presentable.

Focus on doing those activities that you enjoy

Be it playing a musical instrument, reading a book, riding a bicycle or going fishing, do activities that you enjoy and ones which make you happy. Doing things you like will not only boost your self-esteem, and soothe your ego but will allow you to identify your talents and gifts. That will, in turn, bolster and grow your confidence exponentially. You might become famous for doing what you love, but you might not even want to be celebrated at all. Being famous does not make you happy; doing what you love does.

Prepare for the possibility of rejection or setback.

One famous champion once said, "One important key to success is self-confidence. A key to self-confidence is preparation." You need to prepare for the possibility of rejection and setbacks. Why? Because everybody suffers rejection and setbacks at some point or another. No one is exempted. So, the question on your mind, therefore, should not be whether you will be rejected but how you will deal with the rejection when it comes.

Prepare yourself adequately in every situation to minimise the risk and effects of rejection so that your confidence is not broken. For instance, if you land a public speaking role, rehearse what you are going to say beforehand. If you are rejected, do not take rejection personally. Setbacks happen to the best of us; treat them as learning experiences. Learn from your mistakes and move on.

Face uncomfortable situations square in the face.

Running away from uncomfortable situations or people because you feel scared, timid or shy, only reinforces and confirms the shyness. Face the problem that makes you awkward square in the face. How about talking to that person you are afraid to approach? Go on and do it! What is the worst that can happen? Prepare and be ready for any eventuality. This simple yet courageous act makes you an unstoppable bullet train. You start getting comfortable being uncomfortable and begin to feel like you are invincible, and that is the character of someone destined for great things. The more you face your demons, the more you realise you are stronger than you thought and the more confident you get.

Sit up straight and walk tall – you are great!

Start sitting upright and believe you are fantastic. Avoid slumping in your chair or slouching your shoulders. Experts say that posture can not only keep your self-esteem and mood lifted but also leads to more confidence in your thoughts. The way to sit is to open your chest and keep your head level so that you look and feel assured and poised. When you get up, walk like you are on a mission. When you sit up and walk tall, you look more attractive and instantly feel more confident. Try it now; you will feel fierce and confident just by sitting up straight and walking tall.

How do you stop a panic attack?

Panic attacks can be sudden and overpowering. Knowing what to do when they occur can reduce their severity or help stop them. Panic attacks are relatively common, with one article stating that 13% of people will experience a panic attack in their lifetime. People cannot always predict when a panic attack is going to happen. However, planning what to do when it does happen can help. It gives the sufferer the feeling of being more in control and makes panic attacks easier to manage. We will now look at ways to stop panic attacks alongside some general methods for reducing anxiety. We will also look at how to help when someone else is having a panic attack. Panic attacks can create various physical and emotional symptoms. Physical symptoms of panic attacks include:

- Rapid breathing.

- Racing heart.

- Sweating

Emotional symptoms may include:

- A feeling of impending doom

- Intense repetitive worry.

- Feelings of fear and anxiety.

Below are methods that people can use to help regain control and reduce the symptoms of a panic attack.

Remember that a panic attack will pass.

During a panic attack, it can help to remember that these feelings will pass and cause no physical harm, however scary it feels at the time. Try acknowledging that this is a brief period of concentrated anxiety and that it will be over soon. Panic attacks tend to reach their most intense point within 10 minutes of their onset, and then the symptoms begin to subside.

It is important to take deep breaths.

Deep breathing can help bring a panic attack under control. Panic attacks can cause rapid breathing, and chest tightness and can make the breath shallow. This type of breathing can worsen the feelings of anxiety and tension. Instead, try to breathe slowly and deeply, using some of the breathing techniques we covered in the meditation chapter. Concentrating on each breath, breathe deeply from the abdomen, filling the lungs slowly and steadily while counting to four on both the inhale and the exhale phases. People can also try using 4-7-8 breathing, or "relaxation breath." With this technique, the person breathes in for four seconds, holds the breath for seven seconds, and then exhales slowly for 8 seconds. It is worth noting that for some people, deep breathing can make panic attacks worse. In these cases, the person can try focusing on doing something they enjoy.

Try smelling some lavender.

A soothing scent can help relieve anxiety by tapping into the senses, helping the person stay grounded, and giving them a focus point. Lavender is a common traditional remedy known for bringing about a sense of calm relaxation. Many studies report that Lavender can help relieve anxiety. Try holding the oil under the nose, and inhale it gently or dab a little onto a handkerchief to smell. This oil is widely available online. However, you should only purchase it from trusted retailers. If the person dislikes the smell of lavender, replace it with another essential oil that you prefer, such as chamomile, lemon or bergamot orange. You can also keep some close by or on your person if you suffer from panic attacks yourself.

Try finding a peaceful spot.

Sights and sounds can often intensify a panic attack. If possible, try to find a more peaceful spot. This could mean leaving a busy room or moving to lean against a wall nearby. Sitting in a quiet place will create some mental space, and it will make it easier to focus on breathing and other coping strategies. If you or the person has recurring panic attacks, you can carry a special familiar object to help with rounding. This may be something like a small stone, shell, small toy, or hair clip. Grounding techniques such as this can help people dealing with panic attacks, anxiety and trauma.

Try using the 5-4-3-2-1 technique.

Panic attacks can make a person feel detached from reality. This is because the intensity of the anxiety can overtake other senses. The 5-4-3-2-1 technique is a type of grounding technique and a type of mindfulness. It helps direct focus away from sources of stress. To use this method, the person suffering from the attack should complete each of the following steps slowly and thoroughly:

1. Look at five different objects. Think about each of them for a short time.

2. Listen out for four distinct sounds. Think about where they are coming from and what sets them apart.

3. Now touch 3 different objects and think about their texture, temperature, and their use

4. Identify 2 different smells; these could be smells such as the smell of the detergent in your laundry, your coffee or even soap.

5. Finally name one thing that you can taste. Pay attention to the taste in your mouth.

Having completed these 5 steps, the focus has been taken away from the panic and anxiety, and normal feelings should have returned.

Go for a walk or do some light exercise.

A short walk can remove a person from a stressful environment and the rhythm of walking may lead to the regulation of their breathing patterns. Moving around also releases endorphins that relax the body and improve mood. Regular exercise can help reduce anxiety over time, leading to a reduction in the number of or/and severity of your panic attacks.

Try repeating a mantra.

A mantra is a word, phrase or sound that helps with focus and provides strength. Internally, repeating a mantra can help a person come out of a panic attack. The mantra can take the form of assurance and may also be as simple as, "This shall pass", and for some, it may carry a spiritual meaning. Your physical responses will slow as you gently repeat the mantra, allowing you to regulate your breathing and lead to muscle relaxation.

Try out some muscle relaxation techniques.

Muscle tension is another symptom of a panic attack. Practising muscle relaxation techniques may help limit an attack. Other symptoms such as rapid breathing may begin to diminish as the mind senses that your body is relaxing. Progressive muscle relaxation is a popular method for coping with anxiety and panic attacks. It involves tensing up and the relaxation of various muscles. Below are the steps of this technique:

1. Hold a muscle tension for 5 seconds.

2. Now say "relax" as you release the muscle.

3. Allow the muscle to relax for 10 seconds before moving on to the next one.

Now move on to another muscle and repeat the process.

Imagine and picture yourself in a happy place.

Your happy place will be somewhere you would feel most relaxed. This place will be different for everybody and it is likely to be somewhere you feel safe and calm. During an attack, it can help to close your eyes and imagine being in that place. Have calming thoughts about it, for example, you can imagine your bare feet touching the hot, cool sand or soft rugs or cool soil.

Continue taking your prescribed medication.

In cases of severe panic attacks, doctors may prescribe use-as-needed medication. Such medicines usually work fast and may contain elements such as benzodiazepine or beta-blockers. These medications slow down a racing heart and decrease your blood pressure. Valium and Xanax are the most typical benzodiazepines prescribed by doctors. It is important to note that these drugs can be highly addictive and so should be used as per your doctor's instructions. If taken with opioids or alcohol, they can have life-threatening adverse effects. Doctors may also prescribe selective serotonin reuptake inhibitors; these may prevent the onset of panic attacks.

Tell or talk to someone.

It may be helpful to inform someone who may be able to offer some help if your panic attacks frequently occur in the same environment such as a social space or work environment. Let them know what kind of support they can offer. In case the attack happens in a public space, telling another person might help, they may help with isolating you from a crowded place and help you find a nice quiet spot.

Understand and learn your triggers:

You may have the same triggers for your panic attacks such as closed spaces, problems with money or crowds. Learning to avoid or manage your triggers may help to reduce the frequency and intensity of your attacks.

These are a few of the most common types of anxiety triggers:

Caffeine:

In a recent study, people that suffered from panic attacks and social anxiety regularly had a high intake of caffeine. If you have a high daily intake of caffeine, you don't need to necessarily cut down on the coffee or tea, but try to have every other one as a caffeine-free cup. High caffeine energy drinks should be avoided.

Hunger (Skipping Meals):

When you forget to eat, or skip meals, your blood sugar levels drop, this can lead to feeling shaky or jittery and also give you stomach pains. All these can lead to increased anxiety levels. Eating properly not only gives your body the nutrients it needs to function but will decrease the feelings of anxiety that you experience. Food can absolutely affect your mood!

Negative Thoughts and Over-Thinking:

Much of your body is actually controlled by your mind, so when you are feeling upset, the things that you say to yourself can greatly affect your anxiety levels. Always try to focus on a potentially positive outcome of the situation you are thinking about, and look at yourself in a positive light. If you struggle to do this, then try to distract yourself as we mentioned earlier, by doing an activity or surrounding yourself with friends, so that your mind is less likely to wander back to the negative thoughts again.

Social events and going out in public:

Attending an event where you know few or even no other people, is a very common trigger for stress and anxiety. You are not alone, a massive 1 in 3 people suffer feelings of anxiety when in this situation. You have to remember, that no one in the room apart from you, knows that you are anxious. Keep your head up, give people eye contact and say hello as you walk past, even if you don't know them, and your fellow guests will get a sense of confidence and calm from you, which will, in turn, make you feel confident and calm. Try it at your next event, it really does work.

Going out in public can have a similar effect to social events. The thought of a lot of people that you don't know and have no control over, parking or getting into town maybe, queues in shops and what if you can't find what you need .. all these are triggers for panic attacks and raised levels of anxiety.

You can try planning your trip out, so write a list of what you need and from which shops, and have a second option if you can for each item, so if you can't find it here, you can try finding it there. If you're feeling anxious about being late or spending too long being out, then set your parking time to say- 2 hours, or get a return train ticket at a specific time, or book a taxi to take you home, before you go out. You will then know, that whatever happens, you will only be out for a certain time and then you will leave. If you have not managed to find everything you need, then there's always tomorrow or next weekend.

Conflict:

Relationship problems, be it a partner or family relationships, are very common triggers for anxiety and even panic attacks.

If these feelings are overwhelming, then you can try some conflict resolution strategies, such as asking a trusted friend or family member to be present as a mediator, while you talk to the other party to try and work through the conflict.

Often speaking to a therapist or relationship expert can help you deal with the heightened feelings associated with social conflict.

Make a Journal:

If you are not sure what your triggers are or if you have several triggers and you are struggling to work out what's going on, then it is a great help to keep a journal.

You can either keep a pad and pen on you or make a note on your smartphone that you can update easily and quickly.

Whenever you have feelings of stress, anxiety or panic, add a note of where you are, who you are with, what you are doing and how you are feeling. This will not only help you to build up a picture of your potential triggers, but it also has the effect of distracting you from the event that's happening and actually helps to calm you down and remove your focus from the situation. Straight away after you have made the note, either remove yourself from the situation if possible, or take some deep breaths, focus on your breathing to help you relax, and then carry on, with the knowledge that what you have just done will help you greatly in the long run and that you are making positive steps to help yourself.

Effective strategies for reducing anxiety:

Reducing levels of anxiety can help in preventing panic attacks and other related impacts of anxiety. The strategies below may help:

Try Meditation – Meditating regularly is a great way of relieving stress, regulating breathing and promoting peacefulness.

Practice breathing exercises - Slow, deep breathing outside panic attacks is a great relaxation technique that will make it easier to breathe when a panic attack happens.

Speak to a trusted adult – The use of social support can ease your anxiety and make you feel less alone and understood.

Regular exercise – There are wide-ranging benefits of exercise from getting rid of built-up tension, and deeper sleep to generally feeling happier. The endorphins released during exercise will make you feel more relaxed and calmer.

Cognitive behavioural therapy - This is an effective treatment for panic attacks. It gives sufferers the tools to reduce stress and helps to increase their tolerance to feared situations.

Try talking therapy – In cases where panic attacks are regularly impacting your life, you can seek the support of a mental health professional who will provide advice, reassurance and the support needed. These professionals will help you discover the causes and work with you to develop effective coping methods that work for you. The most natural way of combating the effects and causes of anxiety is by making lifestyle changes. The following strategies might help:

• Following a healthy and balanced diet

• Reduce or avoid smoking, caffeine, and alcohol!

• Drink lots of water – stay hydrated.

• Get a good night's sleep.

• Try herbal remedies – these have been used throughout history to treat anxiety and depression. Some of the most popular include kava extract, valerian and pass flora. Try different strategies and discover what works for you, for example, meditation may work well for one person, while exercise may be better for another.

Helping someone during a panic attack:

- If you discover someone is having a panic attack, follow the guidance below to support them:

- Start by talking them through a few of the methods above for instance help them find a peaceful spot, encourage them to take slow but deep breaths and ask them to focus on an object nearby.

- If you do not know the person, it helps if you introduce yourself and ask them if they need your help, ask them if this is their first panic attack and if not, find out what helps them to regain control.

- Remind them that panic attacks never last forever. Do not be judgmental, stay positive and do not validate any negative statements they might make.

- Maintain a friendly, gentle conversation to distract them and increase their sense of safety.

- Refrain from telling them to calm down or telling them that there is nothing to worry about as this devalues their emotions.

- Stay with them however if they feel they need to stay alone then give them space but remain visible.

Knowing when to seek help.

You can talk to your doctor for advice and reassurance if you are worried about a panic attack. Remember panic attacks can be disorienting and frightening. If the attacks are severe and recurring, this would be a symptom of a panic disorder.

Symptoms of a panic attack may resemble those of a heart attack. These include anxiety, chest pain and sweating. You might consider talking to a health care professional if your panic attacks are:

• Getting in the way of your daily life

• They are unexpected and recurring.

• They do not seem to pass with the home coping methods.

•Your health care professional/doctor will discuss your treatment options. If you suspect that someone is having a heart attack or stroke, then that person would need urgent medical attention.

Conclusion

Stress, anxiety and depression should be taken seriously. Loved ones should be able to show their support to their family or a friend with symptoms. People can and will commit suicide because of depression. If you are the one who needs counselling, talk to an expert. Do not let this problem eat you up. The people around you love you and will be there for you when the going gets tough. You also need to help yourself by changing your mindset, eating good foods, and incorporating exercise into your diet.

Always talk to people who understand what you are going through. Never give up. Suicide should not be a solution to the problem. If you feel depressed for almost two weeks, you need to see a healthcare provider now. Life is too precious and should be appreciated. Do not let depression wreak havoc.

Thirty days of consistently moving and doing something about your life problems will impact your life. Make it a happy thing to exercise, change how you think about your life, and determine what contributes to your feelings. It is time that you fight back; regain control of your life. Do not let your symptoms trump a life; it is now or never. It is always necessary to do something about your problem. There are many reasons why depression kills. Do not let this problem control your life. Always look on the bright side of things and ask for help from people. Do not hide in your room, but instead come out and seek a solution!

Always reach out to people.

Stress and anxiety play an essential role in our lives, alerting us to danger or potential situations. We as humans have evolved over our lifetimes to understand and deal with these feelings, and you absolutely can as well. Build your self-confidence, control your brain with a good mindset and meditation, feed your body with essential nutrients, and of course yummy stuff that makes us feel great too, and you will feel in a different and much better place. It may all feel overwhelming, but every small step is an achievement and takes you toward your goal. Take steps one at a time, and focus on only that one step until it has been completed, and then celebrate your achievement, and move on to the next step. Never be afraid to reach out if you need a helping hand, you are not alone.

You deserve to feel confident, happy and stress-free, and you CAN achieve it.

You've got this!

About Me (The Author)

Growing up, I, as many do, went through many stressful situations. Conflicts at school, worries about home and family and financial problems. I was lucky in that I have wonderful parents who knew when to help me, and also when to let me make my own mistakes, to learn and hopefully improve!

This encouraged me to try to find ways to overcome the feelings of anxiety and stress, so I could be able to deal with life in my own way, learning all the time how to become a better and more importantly, stronger, person emotionally.

Nowadays, I am told that if I was any more laid-back, I'd fall over, so something along the way has definitely worked!

Many years ago, I was told about the benefits of meditation and self-help, and it was that that helped me to focus on the positive, and let go of the negative.

With all the things that so many have been through recently in the world, I have chosen to share the advice that was given to me, and hopefully some, maybe many, will find the information helpful to them and help them find the positivity and calm that I am now able to enjoy.

I wish anyone reading this book, all the best health, and positivity they can find. Things WILL get better, you CAN control your feelings and you SHALL succeed.

David. X

This book is dedicated to my son

and my biggest fan.

© Copyright 2022

All rights reserved.

This document is geared towards providing exact and reliable information about the topic and issue covered. The publication is sold with the idea that the publisher is not required to render accounting, officially permitted, or otherwise, qualified services. If advice is necessary, legal or professional, a practised individual in the profession should be ordered.

In no way is it legal to reproduce, duplicate, or transmit any part of this document in either electronic means or printed format. Recording of this publication is strictly prohibited and any storage of this document is not allowed unless with written permission from the publisher. All rights reserved.

The information provided herein is stated to be truthful and consistent, in that any liability, in terms of inattention or otherwise, by any usage or abuse of any policies, processes, or directions contained within is the solitary and utter responsibility of the recipient reader. Under no circumstances will any legal responsibility or blame be held against the publisher for any reparation, damages, or monetary loss due to the information herein, either directly or indirectly. Respective authors own all copyright not held by the publisher.

The information herein is offered for informational purposes solely and is universal as so. The presentation of the information is without a contract or any type of guarantee assurance. The trademarks that are used are without any consent, and the publication of the trademark is without permission or backing by the trademark owner. All trademarks and brands within this book are for clarifying purposes only and are owned by the owners themselves, not affiliated with this document.

David Runacres

Printed in Great Britain
by Amazon